Markeing With Punch

LES BAILEY AND SAM WILLIAMS

Marketing With Punch,
2nd Floor, 46 Banstead Rd, Carshalton, Surrey SM5 3NW
www.marketingwithpunch.com; +44(0)208 915 0650

AVENUE BOOKS

Published by Avenue Books
c/o P.O. Box 2118, Seaford BN25 9AR.

ISBN: 978 1 905575 03 9

Cover photograph of Les Bailey.
All photography by Steve Reeve
<www.stevereevephotography.co.uk>

Printed in Great Britain.

Dedicated to . . .

The millions of business people the world over. May we turn the struggle to survive into the fun of huge growth!

To our wonderful parents Janet and Geoff and Les and Kit.

For all our loyal and brilliant staff at the Parish and Bell Clinic.

To Grace and Henry, we love you very much.

To Connie and Luke; love is not far away . . .

Finally – to the memory of Anita Roddick, an amazing businesswoman. You inspired us all.

A *huge* dedication goes to . . .

*Les Bailey explodes into
"teaching mode!"*

*Sam Williams "wows" a Marketing
with Punch audience*

All small to medium sized businesses whose people attend *"Marketing with Punch"* courses!

Thank you for making it so huge!

Future dates can be found at www.marketingwithpunch.com

CONTENTS

FOREWORD
by *Peter Stringfellow*

There is no doubt that marketing is the new buzzword for anyone in business.

When I first started it was simply called working all the hours that God sends, living, eating and breathing your business. I am asked many times for advice on how to be successful in business. I always give the same answer – "you have to be passionate and want success more than anything else in life". And of course you have to enjoy what you do; that sounds simple, but there are many people making a living by doing something they are not happy with.

It is fair to say that I would not change one day since I started working for myself in 1962. I have been face to face with bankruptcy a few times. In reality there is no formula, you have to make your own way, as I did my way. Believe me, no one can make you successful – that is up to you. So go out there – success is there for the taking, but be ready for a rough ride, with the occasional bloody nose! But at the end of the day you can become a very successful and happy person.

PETER J. STRINGFELLOW

FOREWORD
by *Bernard Hart*
Founder of the "Lonsdale" brand

I was so pleased when Les and Sam asked me to write a foreword for their new book, *Marketing with Punch*, because I know that they have been admirers of a brand that I had the good fortune and privilege to create in 1960 – Lonsdale Sports Equipment, which my partners and I sold out in 2002. I think it is fair to say that Lonsdale is a "Brand with a Punch"!

I was just 22 when I opened the original Lonsdale Shop in Beak Street on the Regent Street side of Soho. Prior to this I had worked for six years (albeit, two of the years were spent in the RAF doing national service) for a well-known sporting goods company near to the City, where I worked with a great deal of enthusiasm. I continually made suggestions as to how the name of the store and the brand could be improved in order to have more impact with the public, but they were comfortable as they were – hence my ideas fell on deaf ears. Overnight – with £250 capital (which I had saved from a short professional boxing career) I decided to form my own business, and I was fortunate enough to obtain the free use of a small (mini actually!) office at a basement boxing gym off Warren Street (just behind Tottenham Court Road) in return for keeping the gym open all day Monday thru' Saturday (the gym opened every weekday evening anyway, but there was nobody there to run it during the day). I decided on the name Lonsdale on account of my interest in boxing (I was fortunate enough to obtain the permission of the 7th Earl of Lonsdale to use the name), and I chose the cinemascope style of logo in order to give the brand an "American" feel. That style of logo was hardly used outside of the USA at the time, but is frequently used now. In my first 7 months of selling my

9

wares from the basement gym I was taking regular adverts in the trade publication, *Boxing News*, as well as visiting boys' clubs and sports clubs in the evenings with two huge suitcases covering a variety of sports goods. One evening I had to stand on an identity parade at Arbour Square Police Station in order that the desk sergeant would tell me where to find the Arbour Youth Club; fortunately I wasn't picked out, and I even got a small order! After 7 months of 'grafting' like this I had the good luck to be recommended to the small premises at Beak Street – just 30 yards from an up-and-coming area called Carnaby Street. After decorating the premises myself in just one week with only the help of a carpenter, I persuaded Terry Downes to open the shop for me; this was most fortunate, because Terry was a household name at the time, and was preparing to challenge for the middleweight championship of the world (it really did mean something at that time), and Terry was both a good customer and a good pal.

On one side of us in Beak Street was HM the Queen's dressmaker, Norman Hartnell, and on the other side was a gents' hairdressing salon. After a short while – and now with two partners – I was able to obtain the hairdressing premises and make it into a second Lonsdale shop. With our good geographical position and strong name with a memorable logo (we called it a trademark in those days) we soon attracted the famous names in sport and show business (sports goods shops were relatively few at that time – for instance, a regular shoe store would not consider keeping "trainers" in stock). At the same time, we took various press advertising (we were placing large adverts in *Boxing News* by this time – something unknown at that time), as well as posters on the underground stations and 'flier' distribution along Regent Street and Oxford Street. By the late '60s we had opened various suburban shops (sometimes in partnership) as far away as North Wales and Norwich, but also in London suburbs (Brixton and Dalston), and at the National Sports Centre at Crystal Palace. We started to promote the boxing brand in the USA in the mid-sixties, and – whether we liked it or not – we found ourselves in the fashion business. This was mainly due to the fact that the practical garments that we designed for boxing training took off as fashion garments, especially the grey fleece garments that we started selling to boxers, but which quickly took off with almost everybody. Our garments were also popular on account of the large 'in-your-face' logo on the front of appropriate pieces. Our hooded sweat-shirts became especially popular, and I have to admit it was Lonsdale that introduced this item to the UK market, but with a genuine training purpose – not as a means of escaping identification. Soon the large store groups came onto us (they had already been 'wrong-footed' by the young entrepreneurs of Carnaby Street in the '60s). Although, at first, we refused to supply, we eventually came to the conclusion that it would be an easier route for us. By the late '70s, we had ceased our interest in retail shops – other than Beak Street (this was the Lonsdale flagship) and we decided to concentrate on wholesaling and licensing (we even had our name over a retail store in Tokyo).

Under its present management, the Lonsdale brand is now worldwide, and is marketed very skilfully and carefully. Personally, I regard marketing as most important to any type of business, and the name of the game is to be original and unique. I must say that some traders do come up with bril-liant ideas, and I never cease to be amazed at names and ideas when I attend trade exhibitions. There is one other thing you need for a small busi-ness – a little slice of luck – which can go a long way!

This all leads me to consider the marketing of the Parish and Bell Foot Clinic, which has been successful because of its originality and bold approach, as well as a competent and technically qualified staff (mind you – there is a demand out there!).

A small fortune must have been spent on advertising, but it has paid off well. When reading the invitation approach of their advert, you are not so likely to be put off even if a longer-than-normal journey is involved. I found it well worthwhile to travel for the sake of my feet!

For anyone with business aspirations I feel certain that it will be well worthwhile and sufficiently entertaining to read and enjoy every word of *Marketing with Punch*.

INTRODUCTION

"There is no such thing as friendly competition"

You want to vastly increase your profits, right? In order to do so, cruel as it may sound, you've got to crush your competitors by using outstanding marketing strategies. **This is the *only* way!**

To pretend to ourselves that we like competition is bullshit. We don't! It keeps us from being filthy rich.

So . . . Who will this book or our courses appeal to?

- *Any self-employed person looking to succeed*
- *Any sized business that wants to grow!*
- *Sales or marketing employees*
- *Shop or store owners*
- *Or anyone that has a product or service to deliver to prospective customers*

What we would like to think is that most of you either want more clients or seek to move from the shackles of self-employed into becoming a 'business'.

When we first started growing our company our turnover was around £1,500 per week. It now averages £60–85,000 per *week* (and rising).

How did we achieve this transformation? **By using the information enclosed herein. It really is no secret!**

Too many people in the self-employed sector, dream of making more money and yet they get stuck doing all of the work themselves and not promoting the business. This is extremely 'average' and not a way to create a *wealthy* business.

IMAGINE IF . . .
Boots the chemist had remained a one man shop? Its success was not until John Boot died and Mr Boot's widow May, and son Jesse turned it into a *company*. Imagine if they had merely worked behind the counter and not used their time to grow.

IMAGINE IF . . .
Richard and Maurice McDonald had just been happy to cook burgers behind the counter and had not used their time to expand?

IMAGINE IF . . .
Richard Branson had been happy to just carry on selling mail order records since 1970?

Can you see what we mean? It's far too easy to get bogged down 'being' your business rather than 'growing' it!

You can't sell a business to investors that relies on *you* to do everything! A great friend of ours put it a lovely way – "If you are captaining a ship you do not do it from the deck, but from the bridge".

> ### *Marketing with Punch's* Golden Nuggets
> Always make sure your company name describes
> what you do, e.g. don't just call yourselves U.P.C., but
> United Plastering Contractors. It gives
> information about you!

This means in reality that you may have to spend all day initially working *in* the company, and evening's working *on* it, (for example planning marketing strategies) but you should aim at a future where you have enough good staff to make yourself redundant. This is not losing control, it's actually gaining control!

Learn how to turn your business around

No one will ever care about marketing your company like you do, so therefore *you* need to learn how best to do this.

We learned the multitudes of marketing methods available today, and along with ethical selling techniques, we became the powerful market leader we are. **In essence we eat our competitors alive by clever marketing!**

Only clever marketing and selling will give you the luxury of seeing your competitors vainly trying to keep up with you.

BUT . . . (there's always a but!) To do this you must keep learning, and constantly putting into use, new and effective marketing tactics. Our courses and this book will give you *stacks* of useable information that will literally kick your business up its profit making arse!

Go ahead – *Market with Punch* and knock your competitors out in the first round!

Alternatively you could always carry on 'plodding' as you are?

Why do we use a boxer as our caricature?

"A boxer is not very politically correct, is he?" we hear you say! No; but then IF you want to succeed you have to think like a boxer and not a quiche-eating new-age queen!

Business is tough – get used to this fact! That does not mean it's not good fun though, and you will get great pride running a successful company.

The lucrative company gets to its customers not by one single source but by multiple marketing strategies.

Similarly, the boxer does not generally down his opponent with a single punch but by a flurry of combinations; upper-cuts, hooks and jabs, parries, blocks and intelligent foot work until he eventually floors his opposition.

As a person marketing their business you will use many different ways to win customers. Like a boxer's punch, some will fail, no matter how good you are; and some will be knock-out blows. The boxer constantly trains and gets faster and more effective. You continuously learn new and better ways to become stronger and more dominant in the marketplace.

By the time the competition attempts to sneak up on you, you are already 50 steps ahead, and in a much stronger position.

THE MORE BRILLIANT IDEAS YOU INTRODUCE, THE MORE YOUR PROFITS WILL RISE. Simple. This is why *Marketing with Punch* **cuts out the waffle and just gives you masses of ideas.**

It is exasperating trying to catch up with a company that keeps growing with new and outstanding business promotion.

Be a Mohammed Ali of the business world. Always different, exciting and f*****g hard to knock down! Having better strategies than other boxers made him not just good, but LEGENDARY. Get the gloves on and let's go and out-box our competition . . .

We want *all* the customers, right?

What makes an entrepreneur?

We have met many great entrepreneurs over the years and the one thing that distinguishes them from managers, accountants, clerks, and all the necessary 'cogs in the wheels' of a business is that they have charisma – charisma by the f*****g bucketload! We have *never* met a boring, 'grey' entrepreneur!

These people have the attitude of Johnny Rotten, a natural rebelliousness that overcomes bureaucracy and red tape and doesn't suffer fools gladly. They have the charisma of Mahatma Ghandi that can move mountains with natural and heartfelt charm. They have the determination of a dog chasing a rabbit. They have the endearing arrogance of Simon Cowell, a 'total bastard' but with caring and honesty to accompany this trait – something you might term 'gentle arrogance'. They have the bravery of a frontline soldier, knowing their next idea could get blown-up, but still soldiering on. They are colourful people who light up a room with mere presence.

The entrepreneur is not a grey-suited 'cardboard cut-out'. Though they wear suits as a cunning disguise, inside they are pure rock 'n' roll, a ticking time bomb, a veritable ball of flame.

These are the people this book and our courses are aimed at. We use masses of brilliant ideas spewed out with passion for what we teach and spooned out with passionate language to follow.

Our pledge is never to bore you with mundane theorising, and best of all, there is . . .

NO WAFFLE!

. . . promise!

Be Outstanding!

Marketing with Punch's Golden Nuggets
"Sell the sizzle not the steak"
Would you sell a steak by telling the story of
how it was slaughtered in an abattoir? Of course
not! We sell it by its taste and flavour using
wholesome pictures!

Whenever you set out to make money from a business you must aim to put something great into the world. Find a product or service that makes people's lives easier or more pleasurable.

When you can accumulate wealth in this way, people will love what you do, speak well of you, and pay you money for doing what you enjoy most.

The great and _loved_ entrepreneurs of this world always aim to do this with every product or service. When these people introduce a new product the public wait with baited breath, knowing it will give usefulness and value.

Creating wealth is easier when we look at every new product or service from the eyes of our consumer.

Firstly look at . . .

- How will it improve their lives?
  That's about it really!

Most importantly

BE ETHICAL ... There are many scams out there in the market place selling useless and unworthy services or goods. You will notice that none of these companies last very long. Some purveyors of these scams or bad services spend their time jumping from one limited company to another, owing money, leaving people out of pocket and generally jumping through legal loopholes.

There is a major disadvantage to this approach. If you spend your time on unethical ventures, you may make money short-term. However, whilst you spend your valuable time working your loopholes, you could be utilising it to bring a brilliant product or service to the marketplace.

In other words, don't fill your days working out scams, it is a waste of time as well as bad for your personal integrity.

NOTE
Our courses are very popular, and we don't allow entry to 'dubious' companies. Individuals wanting to learn the power of our techniques to 'rob' people, will not gain entry – understand?!

Make the business you choose to amass your fortune, *good* for people and enhance their lives.

The definition of "marketing" as opposed to "selling"

Whilst it's true that all our marketing and advertising should be salesmanship in print, the essence of marketing is literally to *pre-sell* your company.

There is a brilliant advert for McGraw Hill Business Publications that sums up what marketing products is all about. It appears in David Ogilvy's excellent book *Ogilvy on advertising* (put this book on your xmas wish list!).

The illustration is of a stern looking managing director sat on a chair facing the reader. Next to it reads:

- "I don't know who your are"
- "I don't know your company"

- "I don't know your company's product"
- "I don't know what your company stands for"
- "I don't know your company's customers"
- "I don't know your company's record"
- "I don't know your company's reputation"
- "Now – what is it you wanted to sell me?"

How bloody brilliant! In other words, the more people know about your business, the more likely they are to buy. People like familiarity.

I have never seen anything sum up *marketing* (as opposed to 'selling') quite so eloquently.

You've Got to Want It!

When we were looking for a new home some years ago we had a budget in mind.

We trawled the internet for homes in our area, and one property stood out from the rest. It was a beautiful double-fronted six bedroom Edwardian house that was naturally out of our price range. We decided to view it and as we walked in the double front doors we were greeted by a huge gallery staircase overlooked by a large imposing stained glass window. We badly wanted that house!

Our wonderful accountant David Blythe, who has been a great source of inspiration and advice to us as a company, nearly hit the roof when we told him of our plans, and emphatically stated we could not afford it.

So what to do now?

We realized we were not going to let this house go, but understood we had to make more money . . . and quickly!

We acquired every great book and audio on marketing. One of us would play the audios in the car or gym and immediately phone the other at the office or write the idea down ready to implement the action. It was a time of incredible growth for us as we put these ideas into action one by one.

The house purchase took around six months to go through as the company grew, and not only did we get our lovely home, but by the time the purchase was complete we had also bought a Bentley Arnage that we had dreamed of owning.

Within a year, we had our home, a housekeeper, an au pair, a chauffeur and tripled our staff numbers. Now we stay at the Dorchester hotel in

London one night a week, own several properties and companies, shop to our hearts' content, holiday when we like, and want for absolutely nothing.

Not only was David Blythe absolutely knocked out at this growth, even the VAT inspector was highly suspicious where this new income had suddenly 'appeared' from, and was mighty impressed when we told her *how* we had grown the company.

With many of us, we need a *want* in order to work harder toward more profits, so it is prudent to set yourself a goal, which may be a certain car, larger home, even more freedom, time for fancy holidays or a villa abroad. Some people dream of early retirement so you may aim to build your company ready for sale as a profitable acquisition.

Do you know how we got to this level? We don't tell you all this to boast about our achievements and look smart, but to point out that we did this by learning the same stuff we teach on our courses, our audios and our books . . . marketing and selling. *Marketing with Punch* will put you on the road to greater profits. We do not offer get-rich-quick schemes, but incredible ways to grow the business you already have to heights you only dreamed of.

Keep that vision, keep your goals and stay hungry!

LET'S GET DOWN TO THE BUSINESS OF MARKETING

Punch

   . . . by punch

      . . . by punch

         . . . by punch

Until . . . KNOCKOUT!!

USPs (Unique Selling Points) and Niche Markets

A niche market is the single easiest place to sell.

What is a "niche"?

You simply carve a place for yourself into a gap in the market. An example of this could be old Bob the plumber who competes with hundreds of other plumbers in the yellow pages and does all manner of plumbing jobs. There's a lot of choice in the market place for this man's services. How about, if old Bob decides to specialise in power showers? His advertising states the luxury of a power shower and the fact his business *specialises* in this area. If you wanted an all-singing and all-dancing top of the range power shower who will you go to? There are millions of plumbers, but only one whose sole intention is to give you a brilliant choice and service *purely* for power showers. It's an easy choice for the consumer to make!

An estate agent may sell all sorts of houses, but one has the prestige of only selling houses over £1m. Where will you look first when your company booms and the family want a sprawling estate? Conversely, the same agent may decide to sell only flats. Where will you look for a flat?

It's all very well being the 'jack of all things' in your trade, but looking for a niche within your industry means more people will trust your expertise in *that particular* field.

This means an easier time for you marketing that entity and a simpler time targeting those particular customers.

23

Think pizza . . .

You have an everyday product like pizza but you require a USP. You need to *stand out* amongst the competition!

This could be done by creating a special rich sauce that people love, and is a secret recipe only available from you. You may do take-away and can offer a 2 for 1 deal on collections. You may even do free delivery by a 'flying pig'!!

The more USP's you possess or can create the more marketing leverage you will enjoy. USP's give you tools to get free PR news stories, and give your advertising an extra 'zing'!

Offer something UNIQUE. A USP is not just a matter of having a low price or anything else 'global'; by this we mean stating you are the best or the biggest. Everyone says *that*! Global statements are simply what every company says about themselves. (Another term for global statements is "platitude" advertising).

When you want to state that you are brilliant at what you do then you let a customer testimonial do this (*see* chapter 16).

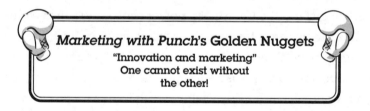

Marketing with Punch's Golden Nuggets
"Innovation and marketing"
One cannot exist without
the other!

Another example of a USP is Bang & Olufsen. Not only do they make high quality audio visual equipment (as other makers do), their whole outer casing is unique and has an incredible look to it.

Bang & Olufsen spend millions on innovation. Not just on the sound or visuals, but they grab people's passionate buying side by creating stunning outer appearance. You don't hide a Bang & Olufsen system away behind hi-fi unit doors, it becomes a rich focal part of your room.

The whole ethos of niche marketing is given to products or services where perhaps there may be a smaller number of people needing it but the niche marketer can target that particular sector accurately and easily!

It's All About Your Customer

People don't generally give a shit about your company's perceived corporate image. What they want to know is, *what's in it for them?*

Rule #1 – love your customer;

Rule #2 – when advertising or promoting a business make it clear what benefits your customer will get;

Rule #3 – do not fall in love with your company logo or name. Customers really don't care about this – only trust or recognition is built by brands – slowly!

There is a van that drives around locally to us that displays a huge name on the side of the van, followed by a tiny 'plastering contractors' hidden underneath. Who really gives a flying f*** that Mr Bloggs is in the van? They need to know that he's a great plasterer don't they?

By all means have a company logo and name but remember this –

- People buy from people (or more specifically what the person can do for them) *not* companies;
- Sell benefits, *not* logos and names (Brand building is secondary);
- Give prospects both barrels about what you can do to make their lives better;
- Being egotistical about your pretty logo and name won't get you a first round knockout when there's competition around and sales to be made.

There's always an exception . . .

The only companies that can literally trade on their name alone are the likes of Virgin, McDonalds, Coca Cola, or IBM. Everyone alive knows what they do. But these guys built their brand *alongside* clever selling over many years.

We assume most of our readers are in growing companies, so stick to telling it like it is, and put your image second. It will build recognition in its own time over many years.

If you are in a high competition business it is imperative that you sell your own individual benefits. If you can offer nothing special or unique you will in all probability merely plod along rather than expand as a business.

5

Let's Look at Branding

Unless your business is a huge multi-national company *don't* rely on branding *alone* to sell your product. Showing off and trying to be clever in advertising while you are small is really not smart.

However, branding can be the adhesive that holds the package together. A logo used as *secondary* prominence in your advertising can give your customers instant recognition.

The secret is to slip your logo into your advertising and marketing materials at the end of a distinctly brilliant piece of *selling* based copy writing.

Creating a brand is important in certain ways and always remember the formula – brand second, but sell first!

Buy or be sold?

Many writers state that people don't get 'sold-to' nowadays, they 'buy' – utter bollocks!

Selling is putting across the message about how your product or service will improve Mr Prospect's life. Brands simply give people auditory or visual anchors of recognition. We still need to *sell*.

Now it's personal . . .

Personal branding can be a major influencing factor and is used to great advantage by the likes of Madonna, the Beckhams, Peter Stringfellow, Bernard Matthews and legions of other entrepreneurs who put their name up for public consumption.

These people are their own outer packaging for their products. In a small business personal branding can be something as crazy as the 'Magic Milkman'. A good friend of ours, Gareth Massey, who has since passed away, was a part-time magician and entertainer. His full-time job was a milkman. This usually involves commission based salary, so Gareth would perform magic tricks for his milk round customers. This got him:-

- more milk round customers;
- spin-off (or 'back-end') work by way of entertainment bookings;
- and *lots* of local media coverage – the press loved the story!

All this took was a bit of thought . . .
On a larger scale of personal branding, look at Bill Gates and how he never shies away from linking his own name to the Microsoft empire. He has two major brands to gain publicity from instead of one. This means that if he decides to start new ventures, he can immediately link the Bill Gates 'fame' to it and gain heaps of free PR!

Personal *and* company brands = more PR! *But* **– what you are *selling* is the ultimate PR!**

Be The First!

Tread the un-trodden path . . . !

. . . or at least make the path look different!

Strong branding has always relied on its product founders to be the first to introduce it or to introduce it in a new way. Did Colonel Sanders invent chickens? Did he shit! Did Colonel Sanders put a whole new slant on the humble chicken? Of course he did!

Have you noticed how many copycat businesses of KFC we see dotted around? Ask yourself, do these copies get the publicity or market share of KFC? In a word *No!*

Think how you can create a whole new slant (or "niche") in what you do within *your* industry.

An easy example could be a hairdresser, who, sick of being one of 65 in a high street, wants a bigger market share. He or she has to *specialise*. E.g. imagine how many people go to the hairdressers for a hair colour? Imagine if one shop *specialised* in this? How many people would be more inclined to trust them to colour hair? The answer is many more, especially those clients who are new to hair dyeing, and therefore nervous of the results.

Don't be too scared of using your 'niche' to *replace* what you do. When we created our own niche, we started it by offering it *alongside* our existing 'generalised' business. That way, if it was going to flop, we still had our existing 'bread and butter'.

Anita Roddick demonstrated an amazing piece of personal branding on the launch of the Body Shop.

The press loved how the busy 'mother of young daughters' set up the whole thing whilst still caring for her children. With all respect for her, she "cleverly allowed the press to 'milk'" this aspect and the Body Shop became glued to the Anita Roddick 'brand' (two brands in one!).

The company is now a global phenomenon with nearly 2000 stores all over the world. The clinch is that as customers, we don't mind shelling out hard earned cash for an enterprise owned by a struggling mother! Brilliant!

On the other hand we find a very similar shop called 'Lush'. The products are amazingly rich, beautifully made and brilliantly presented. Sadly, Lush do not get the same press exposure. Why?

- It's a 'me-too' company in a funny-kind-of-way. It is unique in some great ways, but similar in 'heart' to the body shop.
- They do not have an Anita Roddick to cleverly extract loads of free press coverage!

Big names are generally those who either started the product, or more commonly, marketed the thing properly first time round when their predecessors did not! Think about this carefully, and how _you_ can do this.

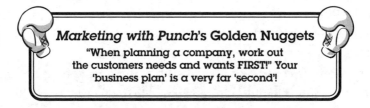

Marketing with Punch's Golden Nuggets
"When planning a company, work out the customers needs and wants FIRST!" Your 'business plan' is a very far 'second'!

Other aspects about a 'first' company to consider are:

- why do people ask for a 'Band Aid' and not a Tesco's plaster?
- why do the 'hoovering' instead of the 'electroluxing'?
- why does any other make of beans except Heinz, seem 'fake'?
- why do the vast majority of people ask for Coke instead of Pepsi?

These products were firsts! They rose and rose rapidly, keeping the competition way behind them.

When you are the first with a product or you can niche a by-product *you* will get the publicity by simply leading the field.

This kind of stuff is what marketing with punch is all about – MAXIMISE YOUR POSITION AND CRUSH THE COMPETITION!

Our own business was copied by two competitors who launched themselves near us in the national press; one even had a celebrity at the helm. The public knew and trusted our regular advertising, and both copy companies disappeared quickly without trace.

For starters our marketing was powerful, our back-up of a genuine product was real, and we have many X factors that keep us No. 1. Well, *you* wouldn't want to be taught how to market *your* business by the 'me-too' people, would you?

WARNING

Provided you have a great product or service people want or need, the techniques in this book and on our courses can achieve growth at a stunning rate.

Ensure you have the resources to handle the increased business.

Introduce these ideas a few at a time and grow slowly. Always test ideas.

Effective marketing *very* effectively pre-sells for you, so be *ready* for growth.

Remember

Test everything – not *everything works* – we all screw up!

All great marketing gurus (including us), have tested ideas we thought were brilliant, only for them to flop!

Look at it from this angle – if we test these ideas, we have a reference to know for the future what doesn't work for our industry.

A boxer learns more from losing a fight than winning it!

Current Customers

We are all guilty of concentrating too much effort into new customers and not utilising the diamond mine that can be our past customers.

Any Marketeer knows it takes more money to get new customers than it does to re-educate and sell new products or services to old/current customers.

Past or current customers know your business, and hopefully you will have taken care of them in the past? You'd better have!

We changed gyms a while ago for no other reason than the new one would 'make a change'. The old gym did absolutely nothing to entice us back!

What could they have done?

- special offer for couples membership;
- extra months on the years membership;
- a free personal training session to ensure we were making the most of the gym;
- a phone call to see if there was anything they could do to entice us back and show they gave a shit why we left!

In all likelihood we would have gone back. Sometimes it doesn't just take a special offer but a commitment to care that brings old clients back to you.

Past customers are far more likely to buy when we give great after-care or service.

When we give great service we can confidently ask new customers to buy from us again, so we have way more leverage when introducing new products and services.

Making existing customers exclusive deals can go a long way to making them feel 'special'. For example, if you sell designer clothes, link to an expensive watch company and organise a champagne reception in your shop where the jeweller has a stand and offers 'specials' to your customers.

Your customer is also in your shop during this promotion, so in all probability they will also buy an item or two of yours.

Think how you can link with a company to promote both your businesses? They call this **'Fusion Marketing'**. It is very popular and highly effective when done properly.

Who can you 'fuse' with to promote both your businesses? Give this some serious thought . . .

The Recorded Information Message

This low-cost and highly effective tool is a multi-edged sword that a huge majority of businesses can benefit from.

Many customers don't have access to the internet or have an aversion to computers but a recorded information message can be your twenty-four hour, unpaid, salesperson. It can convey a lot of information without taking up the time of a sales person and can be an important first contact for people, who, perhaps, don't want to converse with a sales person.

We know it is effective because ours is almost constantly playing!

You have to decide whether a free phone number is relevant to you in this case; an example may be if a small number of high spend purchasers are going to use it. Or maybe you need to educate your customers about what you do?

We get a lot of enquiries, so for our use we simply use a normal area code phone number and publicise that it's *not* a premium rate number (premium rate numbers! have their place but not on your company info line!) The costs involved for a one line set-up are quite reasonable. A phone line which will only take incoming calls, a good quality high usage answer-phone system, and possibly a professional voice-over artist if need be.

Do make your message educational, and appeal to your clients' wants and needs, not your boring platitude-filled 'corporate message'.

This is the kind of garbage to avoid!

"We focus on establishing close business relationships based on giving good quality products at the most competitive price and aim to develop an understanding of our clients needs. Since establishing widgets universal in 1938 we have successfully developed into a broad based widget exporter. We focus on satisfying customer and consumer expectations. We strive to offer a cost effective solution to your widget requirements which is met by a team of dedicated staff, shifting paradigms to outstanding levels of service".

How bloody boring and a brilliant way to say and sell sweet FA!

A better way to entice prospects to listen to your information line is to try the following (or derivations of them).

- don't buy another wobbly widget until you have listened to this enlightening message!
- the 10 mistakes people make when buying replacement nasal hairs
- never over-pay for inferior car valeting again – learn how on this brilliant announcement.

    If you were in the market for these things, curiosity would make you dial the number for sure!

    Don't forget to put 10 reasons why people use your company into the message; *and* here's a clincher. How about asking some of your 'champion customers' to record a testimonial too, you can add this to your message for maximum effect.

The smart bit

The public are notoriously dumb, so *always* start the message with an announcement that *clearly* tells the customer they are through to a twenty-four hour recorded information line, and if they need to speak to someone phone 0077 etc. This is very important as people don't read things properly and sometimes assume that it's an answer-phone they have been put through to.

Use the line to educate your customers *about* your product or service and how it benefits *them*. **Get the important bits in during the first five minutes! Customers may not listen long!**

You can make your message last 20 minutes if you wish. It's been proven *you cannot over-sell a product*.

The major advantages that come to mind with a recorded message are that people trust its content, and it's non-threatening to the caller. It is also working tirelessly for you 24 hours a day. A sales person who needs no breaks, wages, days off or sick pay – *pure genius*!

The script

When you write your recorded message script, as with all your materials, think what it is that your customer wants to *know* (not what you want to 'show-off' about your corporate image!), and, keep it interesting and applicable.

Advertise your recorded message on all your literature; brochures; website; business cards; advertising, even headed paper. Be careful to point out that this is the 24-hour recorded message number *very clearly*.

Let's look at a recorded message script (framework)

- Welcome to Scrivens Building Services 24 hour recorded information line . . .;
- Note – this is not a premium rate number;
- If you wish to talk to an advisor please call our usual number 00770337;
- We assume that you are looking for advice on or about building castles in the sky using prefabricated skyhooks. We have specialised in this unique area for 25 years. Our director is the author of the best selling book "Meeting Clients Sky Castle needs", available from us directly, from Amazon or via your local bookshop;
- With any company you decide to use, you want to know their reputation, so here's a few past clients briefly giving their reviews of our service (2 or 3 clients should now speak giving their full name and area first);

- List publications you have appeared in relevant to your industry. A little tip in this direction – mention magazines, newspapers or TV you have been on or in, even if it was advertising. You simply quote 'appeared in' or 'on'. Many small businesses place a little advertisement in prestige tiles so that they can quote 'appeared in' for marketing purposes (very subtle!!);
- Point out your USPs in a way that is relevant to the clients needs;
- Boast of your unique guarantees;
- Give a brief overview of how your product is made *IF* it's *interesting* and relevant to why yours is better;
- Add the '5 mistakes people make when building castles in the sky';
- Quote the 10 advantages clients get when they use Scrivens Building Services;
- Now walk them hand in hand to the land of how to contact you (phone, websites, emails, etc), plainly and slowly and *repeat* numbers;
- Thank you for taking the time to phone our information line. Any questions you may have, call us on . . .

Use this as a framework, but think how your particular business can 'add on' to this, giving more usable information to educate your customer.

Using The Yellow Pages Effectively (or its Internet equivalents)

As well as the internet, the yellow pages can be a tremendous way to advertise *certain* types of products or services.

It will not suit all businesses, no matter how hard the yellow pages salesperson tries to tell you it will.

Marketing with Punch's Golden Nuggets
Avoid capital letters – lower case is easier on the eye. This applies on signage, brochures, cards and websites, etc.
Avoid light colour print on dark backgrounds for the same reason.

Yellow Pages is great for . . .

- service businesses that supply local areas;
- certain specialist businesses that serve the local community.

Generally speaking certain niche areas would not be sourced within *Yellow Pages*, and if you are covering the entire country, this is an expensive way to go. Our own business is not advertised in *Yellow Pages* as our budget goes on national newspaper ads and internet search engines. In short we are *too* specialist *and* national.

However, most businesses are competing for customers, and the *Yellow Pages* is often the first place people look. For example, we nearly all look there first for plumbers, emergency services, local shops, etc.

Firstly, we want if possible, to be near the first few companies of a particular listing. There is an old trick people use to get these places!

The favourite is to open a limited company called, for example, AAAA and AA Plumbing. This puts you in the first bracket of listings. It is easy to open a limited company in this name and use it purely for this purpose. The name will have to go in the top of your box, but this leaves the rest of your box to fill with copy (along with your proper trading name).

The above is not a new trick, so look at what the competition is doing before you ask your accountant to open a limited company called AAAAAA&A Widgets! Simply ensure you better the existing names!

Hey big boy!

It pays to be big in *Yellow Pages* if your company type warrants this, and where competition is greatest.

The great thing with *Yellow Pages*, like the internet, is no one knows whether your company is big or small by your ad size! Executed properly, a large ad in *Yellow Pages* can increase business dramatically.

Marketing with Punch's Golden Nuggets
Never be arrogant about your product.
A very prestige car dealer in London made
a huge mistake:
We went in to buy this particular car but the
salesman would just not phone us back to finalise
the deal. Our driver accidentally bumped into a
relative of the salesman who, when told he wouldn't
phone back, exclaimed that "he doesn't have to
worry: these cars sell themselves!"
The cars do, the dealer doesn't. We simply went
elsewhere! A lost sale for the company and him.

Creating your larger ad must be congruent with giving better and more relevant information. Don't use the space to put a bigger logo or shout your company name and phone number.

Use the ad to educate your customers about what you *do* and slip in your USP. Add the 24 hour information line, website, free brochure offer, or even better, a free booklet of the '10 mistakes people make when choosing builders'. You have literally got to outsell the thousand other ads around you.

People who consult *Yellow Pages* have no company in mind and need to be drawn to *your* ad. Start with a thought provoking headline. This will immediately stand you out from the competition who nine times out of ten will be logo and phone number based.

Ideas on headlining a Yellow Pages ad

- revolutionary breakthrough in widget supply
- don't make costly mistakes choosing a builder
- amazing . . . free servicing for 3 years
- don't buy an axle sump from a company who won't give you a 100% money back guarantee
- control your building costs easily!
- a 98.95% success rate – incredible!

Make your ad a sunflower amongst daisies!

However, like all advertising, statements made must be genuine, ethical measurable and *true*!

Become An Author

What the 'big players' know

This is our favourite chapter, and one marketing tool that when used to its potential gives you *stunning* credibility over and above your competitors.

Imagine you are obtaining quotes to have your 10 acre garden landscaped. You have chosen 3 companies to visit and furnish their quote for exactly the same service.

All the 'sales people' arrive in nice vans, smartly dressed and all is looking equal.

Imagine you are the client and when the quote arrives from you it includes a complimentary copy of your book 'Amazing landscaping – creating outstanding gardens', along with a covering letter thanking them for the chance to quote, and giving the client a complimentary copy with your regards.

As long as you are not ridiculously over-priced, who do you think has the greatest chance of getting this job?

Your client will be very impressed and realise that you are the one who really knows what they are doing!

We all respect an author and consider them to be the authority on that subject. This is an amazingly powerful tool in your marketing.

We used this in our business and the effect on our credibility was nothing short of incredible! We use the book in all our advertising, website, and brochures. What an investment it has turned out to be!

And – it's easier than you think. Firstly, don't rely on a publisher. They usually offer you 10% on sales, rarely market your book, and withdraw it a few months later.

When you self-publish there are numerous benefits

- your book gets completed quickly
- you aren't waiting around for publishers
- each copy of your book will cost on average £1–2 (if its paperback around 100–120 pages) so its cost effective to give complimentary copies to prospective clients
- you control reprints, so you are not at the mercy of publishers taking it out of print
- if your book can be sold via advertising, the profit margins are greatest
- it's cheaper to send to editors or radio/TV stations for possible promotion
- you control its content and cover price
- it's yours to do what the hell you want with!
- You have *total* control over content/cover/photos/marketing etc. etc.

We sell vast quantities of our books to prospective clients, usually by way of a 'special offer'. This idea gets books sold, and as its primary concern is raising awareness of your business. It is a *brilliant* idea.

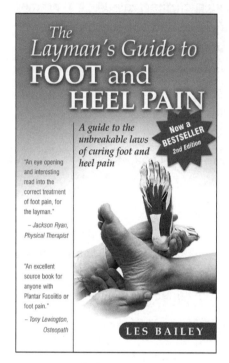

Les Bailey's "Layman's Guide" effectively educates clients, gains marketplace credibility and sells thousands of copies!

We put this ad within our brochure. However, you may like to test selling your book on its own. As you send these out; send out a brochure or information pack separately.

As with any direct selling ad, don't you *dare* advertise it without a special OFFER! Note that we offer a *free* DVD (which is an educational and promotional DVD for our company!) (see later chapter). People love a bargain coupled with a freebie!

And, occasionally we run a special 'low price' offer on the book itself, and *still* include the freebies!

An 'insert' goes out with every clinic brochure to promote the book and its credibility.

However, there is another great use for a book . . . and in reality this is where we are aiming our 'masterpiece'! . . .

Credibility building!

For an industry where there are not multitudes of customers, the credibility authorship gives can be outstanding.

When your book is not needed in huge numbers, most book publishers will produce a small run of books. But remember, you still want it available to buy on Amazon and available to order through bookshops. Your publisher will use a distributor for this.

You are literally using it to 'show off' as an authority in your field. A small run can represent great value for money when your business only merits small runs.

Let's look at some examples of how a book can work to promote your business with titles that impress customers such as . . .

Dentistry
Understanding cosmetic dentistry – a layman's guide to outstanding smiles.

A Builder
House building projects – making your customers project successful.

Restaurateur
See books from the likes of Gordon Ramsey as inspirations, or try titles like:

Amazing Indian Cookery – stun friends with your brilliant dishes.

Car mechanic
Car repair and restoration – outstanding care and service.

Butcher
Exotic meats – preparing and cooking incredible meat dishes.

Motorcycle Dealer
The worlds finest bikes – their care and service.

Insurance

A. How to insure to your customers real needs – an industry perspective.
B. Or – understanding insurance for the layman.

Here we have (A) a *very* powerful credibility builder and (B) a book to entice prospects.

For maximum marketing clout, give a free bookmark that promotes your company!

Spend at least 2 hours working out a title for your book. You will need many titles before you hit your jackpot. Remember to always write your title and back page *before* you start writing. This gives you a guide on what to write and inspires you to fulfil what you promise on the back cover!!

Take time to sit and work on titles for your own industry.
An example could be beauty therapy.

Title e.g. – *Beauty Therapy*
Sub title e.g. – *giving clients that amazing look*
Begin working on titles for *your* book . . .

Title _____

Sub title _____

Title _____

Sub title _____

Title _____

Sub title _____

Title _____

Sub title _____

Title _____

Sub title _____

Title _____

Sub title _____

Title _____

Sub title _____

Title _____

Sub title _____

Title _____

Sub title _____

Note how the back cover of *The Layman's Guide to Foot and Heel Pain* appeals to the lay person and skilfully promotes:

- the author
- the company
- the book

You understand the format by now? Firstly educate and secondly sell your expertise. Use the title to appeal both the book and what you do as a company, professional or tradesperson.

Write, write, write

Writing a book is not as hard as you may think. For the credibility and sheer marketing leverage, it's a piece of piss!

If you don't do grammar and spelling verry weel (haha!) or even if you can't put your thoughts on paper eloquently, you can do the first draft and perhaps pay a local journalist or freelance writer to do the re-write. Ask around, this is not as expensive as it sounds.

As long as you understand your subject, you can research other books when planning your chapter content. Use references when using opinions expressed by other authors.

Don't panic about grammar and spelling in the first draft. It is more important to spew out great ideas for content at this stage. Use photographs, diagrams and cartoons. Along with sub-headings; this helps break up the text into easier-to-read 'portions'.

The book does not have to be humongous in size or page numbers; its effectiveness is in its understandability to your audience be they lay person or professional. And – many people won't even read the book, except the front and back cover which promotes your expertise, trade or company anyway.

A good order of chapters may be:

1. Dedications – you can thank your teacher who taught you your profession, your mum, dad, sister, etc. Try to make these relevant to your image where possible.
2. Foreword – a great idea at this stage is to try and get a celebrity who has used your services or a well known face in your profession. People love to be asked to do a foreword, it's quite an honour! Put the foreword writer's name on the cover for added credibility, for both you and them.
3. *Chapters* – perhaps . . .
    a) Grass roots of widget-making
    b) History of widget-making
    c) Anatomy of widget-making
    d) So what is a widget?
    e) A look at everyday widgets
    f) The shortcomings of general widgets in the market place
    g) Self-help widget-making
    h) The importance of correct widgets, (this is where *you* 'shine')
    i) Summary
    j) References
    k) Your company details – **obviously!!**
    l) Further reading recommendations.

These chapters are only ideas, but may give inspirations for your own chapters.

Writing a book will reap business rewards far greater than the outlay, and depending on you, it may even get you a TV series! Think hard and fast before you discard the book idea. It just could be your goldmine!

Your book can also help others. We produced a charity edition of the *Layman's Guide* where all the profits go to charity.

This gives leverage to get editors to do a story on your book, and helps your favourite worthwhile cause. You are far more likely to get media coverage when a charity is involved!

Get writing!

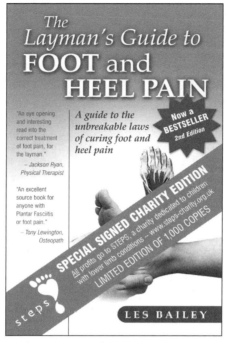

Our charity edition shows a friendly side to our company.

Marriott's Way

I saw a great example of a book used for credibility building. We stayed in a Marriott hotel, and on the coffee table in our room was a book titled "The Spirit to Serve – Marriott's Way". The title sold how the hotel was dedicated to its customers without even having to be read! Brilliant!

Marketing with Punch's Golden Nuggets
Your headline is the most important attention grabber of *any* advertising and *must* work or else the rest of the copy will be *wasted*. Heed this in any advertising!

Copy us!!

If you want to buy a copy of *The Layman's Guide to Foot and Heel Pain*, phone the Parish & Bell clinic on 020 8404 6860 or it can be ordered via your local bookshop or Amazon. It may be useful as a 'framework' for your own book?

Consumer Confidence Versus Price – A Major Fight!

Many businesses make the mistake of selling purely on price. They think all people buy purely on cost.

Of course price can be a major factor, but if your industry is a very competitive one, you must remember to put 'more cheese on the pizza'.

Many customers view service as their major factor in choosing a supplier, and where they cannot see a difference in you and your competitor, a few pounds will surely win the customer over to them.

It is your job to impress the *bejeezus* out of your customers to the point where price is a minor factor. Show your prospects by way of great service, fringe benefits, special bonuses, free gifts, personal service and guarantees that you should be their choice.

Use the marketing advice in this book and price factoring will become less and less important.

A great example of this can be seen in the clothing sector. Marks and Spencer's have always supplied high quality garments wisely sourced and neatly supplied. Giorgio Armani offers shirts at four times the price. He has added *appeal* to his marketing by way of *image*.

Having a Harrods van deliver a fridge that was perhaps cheaper elsewhere shows that people value the added appeal of a particular store's image.

Build on image and service, and pricing becomes less important to almost all market sectors. How can *you* improve *your* image? Brainstorm this *very* important marketing factor long and hard.

Customer After-care

We have found within our own company, and seen in many others, that customer after-care is king. We all want repeat business and referrals right?

Even when customers have experienced problems with our products, the after-care we give has been such that the customers have still referred new customers to us before their problems are finally resolved.

By showing a customer that you care about their problem, and will pull out all the stops for a resolution means the consumer still feels warmth towards your company.

A well written letter or phone call showing genuine empathy and lots of positive messages can be extremely powerful in keeping the customer working with rather than against you.

And the best of this approach is?

- you can truthfully boast of your great after-care in brochures and web sites
- you win over sceptical consumers
- your own feel-good factor comes to the fore
- your company image grows in the consumer's eyes

Brainstorm A "Free Offer"

Many businesses send out a free brochure which is nothing new. These are literally your 'pre-selling' (or a part of it!).

However, it always helps stimulate attention if we attach a 'free offer' as an enticement to get the prospect in front of our sales people. What could you put forward as an enticement to give your *'offer to view your product'* more value?

- *A free 'consultation'*
  useful for medical people, solicitors, or any business where perhaps professional information will be gleaned. These free 15 minute (?) consultations give your prospect a taster of your future service and should leave them wanting more
- *A free 'estimate'*
  a bit time-worn and over-used, so try to give a more 'value added' approach. Let's look at examples of this:
  1. *Car valet*
     A free car grime assessment on leather or upholstery
  2. *Roofer*
     A free pre-winter roof fitness assessment
  3. *Heating engineer*
     A free pre-winter boiler health check

See what we mean? Doesn't 'free estimate' generally sound worn-out? A little thought and brainstorming in marketing can bring floods of great ideas for your particular industry.

One particular idea I like is the 'free booklet', a nice quality 'consumer guide' to your industry. To be effective, these must be genuinely helpful to the client. Ideas like 'the 10 mistakes people make when choosing a chocolate teapot', (If chocolate teapots are your industry?) or an information book on caring for your heating system, car engine, carpet or dog. The permutations are endless.

These cheap-to-produce booklets have appeal in that they are free, and give useful information. Ever since the advent of the Royal Mail, food companies have given away recipe booklets with information on cooking with their product. It's not a *new* idea, but one that is seldom used as businesses forget its power!

These booklets give a nice helpful impression of your company and encourage people to use more product!

The net result is that your tips booklet teaches your prospect the basics of care; but when things go really tits-up call us and we will fix/clean/refurbish it as only a professional can!

Coupons

A coupon can be effective in tipping people over the edge to buy your product and 'save' money (prospects fear losing what they have got more than they care about ways to gain!).

However, we must take care not to appear desperate or cheapen what we do with a tacky coupon. As the old saying goes "cut your cloth to match". In other words you wouldn't use a supermarket-type 'money off' voucher for a Rolex watch specialists!

However, if your business is of the type that "piles 'em up and sells 'em quick", use a simple coupon, it's easy to understand.

Another approach if you are upping the image stakes is to perhaps use a certificate type voucher which may take the form of . . .

- Chiropractor – initial assessment of 15 minutes , free of charge
- Mechanic – free 10 point engine check
- Beautician – a free skin assessment
- Dry cleaner – a free item such as a shirt 'to give your quality a test'

- Valeter – free leather treatment with each valet, or one seat done free as a trial (who's not going to get the rest done?)
- Newsagent – 3 free days delivery 'to test your great prompt service'

Now assess how you can entice customers to your business with a voucher . . .

There is a golden rule with vouchers . . . you absolutely, completely, emphatically, really, really, must put a perceived value on your voucher, e.g. free assessment worth £35!

In our business we use *The Layman's Guide to Foot and Heel Pain* as a freebie, and the best part is it's worth £9.95 to a consumer.

Using this approach gives your coupon 'credibility'. You can pass these to your existing clients to give to friends and family. You can give these vouchers to another local business in exchange that you promote theirs.

These vouchers must be a lead on to a sale in a relevant percentage of cases. If this is not happening either vary the voucher type or abandon ship if the results are really poor! Remember, in the world of marketing all you can do is test, test, test. Nothing is cast in stone.

Do a small tester run relevant to the size of your company so that you can gauge response before you print 50,000 and find out it dive bombs!

Use A 100% Money-back Guarantee

Many companies are in industries where people have 'seen it all before'. People are afraid to commit money for fear of looking stupid when the item fails to work or breaks down. There are a lot of sceptical prospects out there!

We know of a company where their product is 2–10 times higher in cost than similar products the customer had bought from other companies where the product failed. Imagine trying to sell in this environment? However, the company enjoys a success rate of well above 95%, but more importantly they offer a *100% money back guarantee* that their version will work. Without this guarantee it is estimated that sales would be at least 80% lower than they are.

People trust a genuine money back guarantee, and this should be shouted from every piece of company literature. Use it in brochures, advertising and mail shots. It can be a huge sales clincher!

Obviously this is not for *all* businesses, but if you can find a way to utilise this approach, the rewards can be amazingly powerful.

The amount of guarantees you will have to honour will be minimal compared to what you can make financially from giving it as an enticement.

A little secret to guarantees is to offer them for life where possible and practicable. If the guarantee is for a limited time people will rush to return the item by that date. People will generally put off 'until tomorrow' when returning items.

We will let you into a little secret . . .

In the UK, if an item or service is unsuitable for use, the customer is entitled to their money back so capitalise on this law!

Therefore, it makes sense to use a guarantee in your selling literature. It gives the back-up that you have confidence in your goods and have the guts to honour this with your guarantee.

You may need to run tests on your guarantee and how you offer it, and furthermore, avoid putting too many unfair conditions attached to it. The more user friendly the guarantee is the more 'customer-loving' it becomes. More customers will flock to you.

Remember, that a guarantee won't just gently trip people into buying, it will automatically give them a safety net to feel secure doing business with you.

One useful tool you may use in certain service or 'non straightforward' items is to prepare a *guarantee contract* that sets out conditions, and get the customer to sign this. Examples of this may be . . .

- Installing a boiler – obviously these are never straightforward and may take a little adjustment on your part until perfect. The customer should sign for a certain number of 'boiler adjustment visits' so they understand this
- Medical – again never straightforward. Like the boiler, 'little tweaks' may be necessary in certain procedures.
- Car repairs – same scenario as above.

Think about your business and how much "tweaking" can be needed on your goods or services before setting out the guarantee conditions. It can be sensible to get a lawyer to help you draft a contract to ensure all is legal and fair to both the customer and you.

Marketing with Punch's Golden Nuggets

Keep your staff trained.

Sales and specific industry training is a must just as marketing training is. Invest heavily in training. It will pay dividends! Look out for future marketing with punch products and courses!

Create A Charity Alongside Your Business

This really is a win-win situation and is something you can add to your marketing repertoire as you grow.

This is not something to do in the very early stages of growth as it can be time-consuming. However, after using the information in this book you won't be a small business for very long, will you?!

Why do we call this a 'win-win' situation? Simply your company will win by creating a caring and giving image, and secondly the charity wins by getting more funds!

Where possible find a cause that may be associated with your type of company. Some obvious examples are a kids clothing company may support a kid's charity; a pet shop can raise funds for an animal charity, etc, etc.

If you cannot find an 'allied cause' almost any charity can do with your support, and will shine a favourable light on your enterprise.

There are two approaches to allying a charity with your business:

- you can start your own charity. This is for the larger company, e.g. if you run Dicky doo da's Donuts, you may start the Dicky doo da's Donuts Foundation for Children. You can then be seen to actually have a charity as *part* of your company,
- *or* the small business can be linked to a charity e.g. you may get staff and customers involved with raising money for an *existing* charity. (Choose a charity that does not make you donate a minimum amount before 'allowing' you to help them!!)

The second approach is excellent in that it is not too time consuming with the setting up of a charitable trust.

The actual raising of funds for charity can be done in a number of ways:

You can involve your staff in sponsored walks, runs or even slimathons (don't, for f*** sake, ask female members of staff to 'slim for charity' or your life may rapidly draw to a close!!!).

How about getting your staff involved in a sponsored version of your company's actual service?

Ideas for this could be:

- a car dealer – a round the clock country drive;
- a cleaning company – a sponsored clean on a new charity's premises or a popular public building;
- dog walking service – sponsored dog walk;
- sports shop – sponsored run or walk;
- marital aids shop – a sponsored f ["*Enough of that please*" – *the publisher*].

You should always have collection boxes in your premises collecting for your chosen charity.

A great idea is to get your best clients involved, especially if the event gives an excuse to socialise with them and build better relationships.

Attempt to raise as much money as possible from the event, and let the press know prior to the occasion and afterwards. If the press are going to cover it, it *must* be newsworthy.

A warning – if we hear of any of our readers or course attendees doing something as unimaginative as sending the media a picture of 2 'suits', one handing an oversized cheque to the other (complete with cheesy grins!). We will be mighty pissed off! Use your imagination and make the story release irresistible to a journalist. In other words make them really *want* to write about it.

Ensure you let all your prospective and past clients know you are doing the event by adding it to your website, mail shots, recorded messages, brochures, in-house magazines, etc.

And finally, don't forget to produce a limited edition of your new book for charity, and *donate 100% profits to it!*

***Marketing with Punch*'s Golden Nuggets**
Make wording (regarding your business) on
advertising and brochures etc so strong that to
use your competitors would seem foolish. Do
this subtly!

16 The Awesome Power Of Testimonials

In short, a testimonial is an approval of your business by a satisfied third party (financially unlinked) that greatly reduces your prospective client's perception of any risk of doing business with you or your company.

Think about that for a moment. . . . Analyse the above statement and perceive its sheer power.

Many businesses have the problem that prospective clients have used other businesses in the same industry and enjoyed less than impressive results. They are rightly sceptical.

Use testimonials from the word 'go'. Your advertising, where possible, should be one large testimonial from a past customer.

Your brochure should be peppered with testimonial extracts. Your book should have testimonials on the cover, and your shop or office should be a display board of testimonials.

Put testimonial binders on your office coffee table (and remove magazines or newspapers so that customers only have these to read).

Frame testimonials on your wall where customers see them.

Have a section easily opened by a 'click' that displays all your testimonials on your website. The most powerful way to do this is to lead in on your home page as '100 amazing client success stories – click here'. (We display the testimonial letter 'as it arrived' and just blur the address and phone number. This is more powerful than merely printing it in the same font as your website.)

. . . and, best of all . . .

Sent with our own brochure and book, and playing in our office, is a visual presentation that is peppered with successful past clients. We send these out on DVD, which after the initial cost of filming is a very cheap thing to do. It's a wonderful way of netting our 'not yet' clients by using old ones to say how wonderful we are!

We can pontificate all day about how great we are as a company, but when someone else unrelated financially or otherwise tells our prospects how great we are, the selling leverage is incredible.

> **Marketing with Punch's Golden Nuggets**
>
> All your staff must market for you. Teach all of them your strategies, USP's and services. Keep them a part of your marketing team; from telephonists to handymen and cleaners.

If you want to economise on brochure costs, one way to do a great send out is a smaller brochure and a *pack* of copied testimonials. You would usually blur the addresses/telephone numbers, but certain *champion clients* may be happy to accept phone calls from your new prospects.

We can see this working well for builders, estate agents, certain health and beauty sectors, and any industry where there is a wide chasm between quality operators and cowboys!

A further positive aspect is that the customer is reinforcing in their own mind how great you are, and the mere fact of writing this on paper is magnifying and implanting this in their memory.

Get those testimonials in

Many of you have great quality, high value businesses, but never get testimonials?

You will be pondering how to get these in the letterbox! This is usually easy if you strike quickly. When a customer thanks you for a job or product, ask them immediately for a written testimonial. 99% will say yes!

Another way to get them to take action and write testimonials is to offer an incentive for genuine letters. It could be based on this type of layout:

Now **we** need your help, and **you** can benefit too!

All of us at D.G. Widgets get great satisfaction from solving your difficult skyhook building needs.

Our after-care service is free of charge and our dedicated team are always on hand to help you if needed.

All we ask of you

You have very likely read all of the testimonial / thank you letters on our website and in our waiting area. These were all from satisfied customers just like **you**.

All we ask is a similar letter from you that states how we helped you, why you chose us and what you liked about our service and product.

How do you benefit?

We put your name in a hat and every 4 weeks we randomly draw a name out. The lucky winner receives a Rolls Royce Phantom and a night out with any supermodel of their choice (or 6 free National Lottery tickets!!). Your name stays in the hat ad infinitum so you *never* lose the chance to win.

Very best regards

	D.G. Widgets
	17 Uxbridge Road
The team at D.G. Widgets	Clacker Street
www.dgwidgets.com	Snickleborough
01707 47360074	DS10 3SU

An approach such as this can be very effective at bringing in those valuable testimonials.

Always try to give a *worthwhile* prize (maybe the Rolls Royce is a little *too* worthwhile!). If you want to put those testimonials to use marketing, you must get a release form signed if you are going to use the client's name.

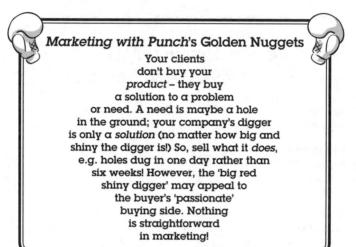

Marketing with Punch's Golden Nuggets

Your clients
don't buy your
product – they buy
a solution to a problem
or need. A need is maybe a hole
in the ground; your company's digger
is only a *solution* (no matter how big and
shiny the digger is!) So, sell what it *does*,
e.g. holes dug in one day rather than
six weeks! However, the 'big red
shiny digger' may appeal to
the buyer's 'passionate'
buying side. Nothing
is straightforward
in marketing!

Testimonial marketing is a real clincher. In advertising it's de rigeur for making it work. Where possible, all advertising must be testimonial-based and made to look like a news story in the same style and font as the publication you are in (or as near as editorial will allow).

Test it, use it. It's appealing to the *people just like me* mentality of your prospects.

One pointer we tested was a celebrity testimonial. People assume celebs are paid for these and take it with a pinch of salt. AVOID!

This was our own celebrity advert that failed abysmally! (No fault of our celebrity).

The exception to this is if a celebrity is used in a PR article or story. This gives a whole different perspective and works very well. Celebrity testimonials will not *always* work as we hoped in advertisements, but can do wonders for your company's credibility on websites and in-house publicity material. For example, video footage, brochures and testimonial letters.

HEEL PAIN – SNOOKERED!!

When world class ▇ was suffering from excruciating pain in the heel and arch of his foot he spent 10 and a half months trying every conceivable method of treatment available.

The pain, which began last January, started to affect his whole life, walking was unbearable and everyday activities were becoming a chore. Eventually the pain was so bad that he was unable to practice his beloved snooker, or even relax away from it all playing golf. His young son could no longer understand why dad could not play a game with him either. The pain, which turned out to be Plantar Fasciitis (commonly known as heel spur or policeman's heel) was excruciating and frustrating. He was referred to countless medical consultants, was injected with cortisone, tried physiotherapy, osteopathy and acupuncture all to no avail.

Free consultation

Eventually a friend gave ▇ an article about a clinic called Parish & Bell who specialised in heel pain. "I had suffered for over 10 months and tried a lot of treatments but thought I would give it one last try and phone them for an information pack!" explains ▇

▇ found the guide to be very informative, this clinic were the only specialists in heel and arch pain outside the USA. He decided to travel to them for a free consultation to assess whether they would be able to help him.

▇ found a cure for his heel pain was right on cue at the famous Parish & Bell Clinic!

The clinic, which was founded by Les Bailey a former osteopath and author of "The Layman's guide to foot and heel pain!" a best selling book on foot ailments explains, "I had foot pain for years in my twenties and despite working in the medical profession as an osteopath I could not find one colleague or practitioner who could alleviate the pain. This sent me on a mission to find a cure for my pain and help others.

One Visit

"Over the years we achieved this in the shape of the 3D optical foot scanner and now 17 years on with this accuracy and skill we can offer patients a 100% money back guarantee to clear their heel pain as well as a 98.95% success rate".

▇ attended the clinic in September and

Heel pain banished: ▇ found the answer in Orthotics made using a 3D optical scanner (above)

saw Paul Williams, one of the clinics highly trained expert biomechanical consultants. "I was extremely sceptical!" explains ▇ "If all the previous practitioners I had seen before could not help me, how would this guy?"

98.95% success rate

Paul diagnosed the central biomechanical cause of his condition and decided the clinic's highly specialised orthotics would give the desired effect and clear the pain he was experiencing.

His feet were scanned on a 3D optical foot laser, which takes 64,000 measurements per 2.5cm of foot. The scan, which goes to America via computer, allows the technicians to produce the orthotics to an accuracy of +/- 1/1000th of an inch.

"When the orthotics arrived I was amazed at the results!" says ▇ "Within two days of receiving them I was totally pain free".

▇ has been able to quickly resume

playing snooker and golf, and even walk on his marble floors free of any discomfort.

Paul, ▇ "saviour" explains, "Having the luxury of specialising in this niche area, as well as using unique materials and the most up to date technology allows us to achieve amazing results for our patients. We receive patients from all over the UK and Europe and have helped them achieve the same relief as ▇

Many patients who consult us have tried all manner of treatments and have suffered up to 40 years before finding a cure so being able to clear their pain usually in one visit is a wonderful feeling for us and makes our job very worthwhile.

Painless procedure

▇ adds, "I am so happy with the results, I will definitely be recommending their treatments to anybody with foot pain". The clinic also treats a variety of other foot complaints including pains in the ball of the foot, ankle pain, Mortons Neuroma and shin splints. They can also prescribe specialist models of orthotics including sports, golf, hiking, slim fits and many more.

The cost of treatments can vary in price as the orthotics are individually made, but the consultation is free and only one visit is usually ever necessary.

Ecstatic Customers

We want to provide such great products and service that customers will tell everyone!

Is this obvious or not? We don't just want customers to be pleased with our company's efforts, we want them dancing over the moon!

It may be stating what is blatently true, but please don't sell or offer inferior products or services if you want to get steadily more wealthy from your endeavours.

You will get away with this for a short while but it is not the key to long term company growth.

Have you ever seen a crap company get *really* wealthy? No, nor have we!!

So ensure your business has an extra factor that knocks your clients socks off.

The simple magic in this is to give more or better than others in your sector, and then by way of marketing, let your prospects know about it!

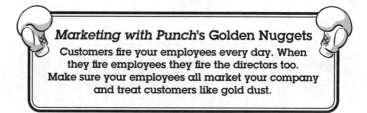

Marketing with Punch's Golden Nuggets
Customers fire your employees every day. When they fire employees they fire the directors too. Make sure your employees all market your company and treat customers like gold dust.

A great example of this was a company called Permaguard who I called in to apply a special finish to our best cars.

It is not a cheap service, but the technicians worked really hard on the job and gave great results. The 'X' factor that made us into lifelong clients was that while the technicians worked on the best cars, the boss personally cleaned our land rover at no cost!

That 'little extra' paid dividends for Permaguard.

18 Thank You, Thank You

Our own consultants, upon completing a deal, habitually send their customer a thank you card.

Remember that any business transaction can lead to referrals, and a simple thank you card heightens the customer's perception of you and your company.

It is not expensive to have these printed with your own wording branded with your company logo, etc. But if you are starting out and budgeting, simple ready made cards arc ok.

May I thank you for choosing Mrs Hubbard's Widget Co. for your new widget extractor.

We value you greatly as a customer and look forward to helping you again in the future.

Should you experience any problems please contact us immediately so we may remedy these.

Remember we are with you every step of the way!

Wishing you many years of happy widget extracting!

Kind regards

P.S. All the best with the new baby!

Bob

The advantages of a thank you card

- destroys post-buying remorse in 90% of cases
- makes the client see you as a 'person', and people buy 'eye-to-eye' from people, not companies
- they oil the wheels for referrals and repeat buying.

The disadvantages of a thank you card

Err? Don't know sir . . .?

The 'clinch' of a successful thank you card is the following which you absolutely *must* do.

- always write the address on the envelope by hand
- you must put a personal message inside it to acknowledge you see the customer as a person and remove the corporate identity of the card. For example, you may have gleaned from the client little details such as:-
  - A new baby on the way?
  - An important birthday?
  - A sporting event?
  - An operation they may be having?

Put this in a p.s and wish them luck with it (or any appropriate message). This works a treat.

This approach is mighty powerful and tells your clients that you appreciate their custom and that you have listened to them as people.

You can even send a thank you card thanking people for allowing you to quote for a job. Thank them for their time in this respect. (This may also be an appropriate time to send a complimentary copy of your book?)

Whatever you do, do not forget the "p.s" bit. The personal message boosts the thank you cards power tenfold.

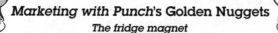

Marketing with Punch's Golden Nuggets
The fridge magnet
If you run a local service that you want people
to access quickly, use a fridge magnet as well as
a business card. These are so regularly and
easily seen on the prospects fridge and are
rarely discarded.

Complaining Customers

Unfortunately customers nowadays are mentally fed on a diet of negative consumer programmes on TV, as well as 'Trading Standards', 'Consumer Direct', etc and this has led to the breeding of the 'customer from hell'.

It seems everyone wants a slice of compensation, refunds, free stuff, etc. etc.

However, ask yourself firstly *why* they complained. Is your product or service *really* shit or are you not giving good aftercare? If so, take it on the chin, you deserve it!

Generally people complain because they believe in us. They see us as being able to do something about it.

Beware of the client who unhappily slopes off into the loving arms of your competitor.

When you get a complaint it should be dealt with by a director or senior person.

One of the most amazing stories of how a complaint had been dealt with was to the clothing designer Paul Smith. One of the staff at his Milan branch had apparently been very arrogant and rude to the customer and they felt the company should know. They wrote a simple letter to the manager at Paul Smith's HQ and within a matter of days Paul Smith himself was on the phone apologising for the standard of service. He was genuinely mortified. Now *that* was impressive!! And yes they do still buy more of his clothes. Why? Because he showed he actually cared personally.

Useful positive messages from a director to a customer in times of complaint can be:

- asking if they would mind working *with you* so the problem can be rectified
- assure them you are on their side
- and 100% **mean it**!

Don't bullshit customers! If you promise to do something – do it! People see through soothsayers and you will lose that customer and all possible future referrals.

A complaint can give you the opportunity to show off how *great* your company actually is, so use the opportunity and don't take a complaint personally.

Another great way to establish rapport with the customer is to ask them as an 'outsider' their advice on how you as a company could do better.

You have just turned your complainer into an unpaid consultant!

This free information could help you establish better ways of doing things. You then send them flowers or similar as a thank you for their advice and time.

Hey Presto – from complainant to fan! Another win-win situation!

Marketing with Punch's **Golden Nuggets**
Work out 'customer worth' to your company.
A hairdresser whose client spends £80 12 times a year is worth £960 annually. Twenty of these are worth 20 x £960. Keep these people and market to add more of them *constantly.*

Referrals Cost Nothing

When a happy customer or client refers a friend, colleague or family member to your business they are your unpaid sales representatives!

Sales reps are expensive to employ, but these references cost you nothing and have a major advantage.

A sales rep is with a customer to earn him and his company money. People know this.

A referring customer approaches your prospect unbiased financially, and exclaiming what a great job you do. Mr or Mrs Prospect is far more likely to act on this than on a sales rep.

What we need to do is get our ecstatic customers in the habit of referring, and make it worth their while.

The easiest way is when you have done a great job; ask there and then if they know of anyone else who could use your services. Too many people are shy to ask customers this and miss out on masses of referral opportunities! They may give you numbers or you may give them cards (or your book) to pass on to likely future customers.

People love to tell others of the great service they had.

There are times where a 'special thank you' for a referral can be optimised. You may send certain presents to show your appreciation, these could be:

- flowers
- theatre tickets
- restaurant voucher

- champagne
- hotel voucher.

For larger contracts that will net you huge profits, even something like a watch is lovely to receive and will make the person feel like sending you more referrals.

Do make these a genuine *thank you* and not a *bribe*, so send gifts *afterwards*!

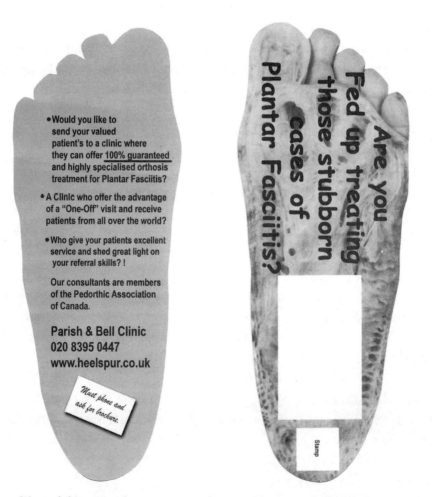

We used this approach to encourage other practitioners to send referrals to us.

When you get business via a referral source, you will be amazed how much easier it is to sell. There will be far less resistance regarding price. This also works to a slightly lesser extent by using testimonial marketing (see relevant chapter).

The obvious psychology of the referral is that the subject already knows you deliver what you promise, as their friend/colleague/family member has tested you. This avoids them 'taking a chance' on you when dealing with a 'new business'.

One system we have used is to give our clients a voucher in the form of a postcard, this entitles the receiver to a free copy of the book.

The Free Book voucher enables people to pass on our company details in a 'value-giving' way.

How this works so well is that our book is also a powerful tool to bring customers in.

However, the voucher has a perceived value of £9.95 which people love to give their friends and family. And the best of it is that people won't waste time or a stamp unless they really want it. If only one in four people visit us after reading it, this has cost us around £5 to net a prospective customer.

Another approach to try is a postcard that says if you send us a referral who uses our service we will donate £X amount to their chosen charity and allow them to buy a second widget at just over our own cost price. It can be advantageous to do a deal on this with your suppliers as you can both reap the rewards!

There are many variations on this theme; you merely need to tap into what it is your business can do and what your customer wants or needs.

Always try to ensure that you subtly introduce the fact you like referrals early on in the business relationship.

Cross referral

By cross referral we mean 'business to business'.

For example, an estate agent may refer removal people, surveyors, lawyers, builders or mortgage brokers.

Many businesses have the potential to refer or be referred.

Tyre shops may refer or be referred by mechanics or car dealers. In cases like these, reciprocity is the "lubricant"!

Ensure your referral sources are fully au-fait with your type of work, so you may have to do a freebie job for what will become a great referral source.

Some industries find that a 100% refund for customers who refer them X number of clients works really well. This can be powerful in the right business sector. To get the best from this put a time limit on it, or people just drag their heels!

A joint marketing venture can be a great way to go, and, described in a nutshell, involves a swap of space either on internet sites, company publications or brochures. You can even do a special offer to your joint marketing customers, and in turn they carry your special offer. Obviously you need to use a company who have a link to your industry.

"Link" examples could be:

- plumbing supplier – wood or builders merchant
- dentist – doctor
- bookshop – college
- car dealer – valeter
- 4x4 dealer – off-road driving centre
- gym – clothes shop

There is little point joint marketing with unlinked companies. There is no mileage in linking your gym with a working men's drinking club! However you would wish to link to a local golf club or sportswear shop! Use your head and some great links will come along.

Lead sharing can be particularly effective. For example you may be a retailer dealing in safes and physical security. Your lead swapper may deal in alarm systems and CCTV. You simply swap customer name databases and give a 'special offer' as customers of each other's business.

'Crafty' referrals

An easy way of obtaining a 'referral without a referral' is, for example, the window cleaner who is cleaning the windows at no. 20, puts a note (preferably handwritten?) into the homes around it telling them they are available to do theirs and will give a half price first clean to introduce themselves.

Office cleaners may put a note on the desks of other businesses in the same block using the same approach as the window cleaner.

The 'crafty' referral is an 'implied' referral and does not rely on you waiting to be referred.

Another quite common but very effective version of this is one used by builders or refurbishment contractors whilst active at a property. This method is particularly good as its implication is that the client is 'proud' to have them there.

The wording on these boards could read similar to the following:

Another useful manoeuvre for businesses working on homes or business premises is a postcard written thus:

We apologise...

We are doing work at no **74**. There may be some noise and temporary mess in the road.

Please excuse us for this, we hope to finish very soon.

If there are any problems regarding noise or disturbance please telephone us on 01777 822223.

Assuring you of respect to our client's neighbours.

A&A Builders, 74 Notty Ash Road, Croydon, 01777...

WE DO CARE. Your contact's name is

....

What a lovely company, eh?

This could be used by landscapers, double glazing installers, gardeners, roofers, pavers or even property developers. There doesn't have to be noise or mess!

Neighbours are astounded and rightly impressed at your company image and professionalism.

The handwritten number will help ensure it doesn't get thrown away as 'another bloody leaflet', so print on both sides of the postcard.

Can you think of 'crafty referral' techniques for your business? There are many angles on this one that multitudes of businesses can use.

Let's personalise referral

Whatever business you are in you can personalise a few of these to suit your industry. Don't get blinkered, we have only given examples used by these particular types of business.

- SMALL SERVICE INDUSTRY (hair salon, beauty parlour, remedial massage, nail bar, sun bed shop, etc)

  We encouraged a local beautician to do a thank you letter to customers who had referred a new face to them.

  In the thank you letter she simply enclosed a lottery ticket which was very well received by her referee and cost her a measly £1!

  A coupon or referral card is dropped at local hotels/guest houses or even clothing shops. The member of staff who gives a certain amount of referrals receives a free treatment or haircut. If you want this to be successful you must put a perceived value on the service or it becomes just a worthless token, e.g. a hair styling appointment worth £45?

- INTERIOR DESIGN SUPPLIES – (construction supplies, furnishers, carpet shops, etc)

  Get to know the people who quote for home/shop work such as architects, surveyors, property maintenance contractors, etc. When these people get involved with a job, ask for the clients details and send out a special offer on supplies.

Another way to do this is to find out from local papers who is applying for planning permission for extensions etc and write directly. You must have a special offer or USP to give or these will merely end up in the bin.

- SPORTS FACILITY/CLUB/PIZZA SHOP (!)

The tactic I love for gyms (and this can be used for all types of business) is where your ad may say along the lines of – Do you have a current gym membership anywhere in the area at any gym? Membership close to running out? Bring your membership card to 'our gym' and receive a discount on membership/free tracksuit/kit bag – choose what to offer! It's a powerful motive to switch gyms to yours.

This can also be used by, for example, pizza outlets where you do a special offer on presentation of one of your competitor's menus or flyers.

Another method which has much going for it is where you give free trial vouchers for members friends or family to discover how great your place is and it costs you sweet Fanny Adams! Maximise effectiveness by making it a one-off visit which the person must register for (so you can phone and mail shot them) *and* put a time limit on it which should be hand written in *pen* on the voucher.

If your clubs activity involves costly materials (perhaps clay pigeon shooting or anything where expensive consumables are used) you may have to screen potential triallists, or perhaps make a charge for the consumables only.

Ideally you want triallists to be local in cases of a local business, so you may have to form a registration to ensure this?

Where you wish to ensure that only financially viable people try your product or service you need to link with a company of the same calibre.

For example, we receive the Bentley Cars Magazine, a beautifully produced high quality publication. Inside this are adverts for private yachts, investment banking, 'top drawer' jewellery, etc. that would be useless advertising in *The Sun* newspaper or *Take a Break* magazine!

If you were going to encourage test drives at your Ferrari dealership you would avoid the local free paper or you would be crammed with time wasters and dreamers!

Worded well, these referral vouchers can have an effectiveness rate of 30–40%. Test this and see how your own business can benefit.

Results can work out that of 200 vouchers, perhaps 100 will try the offer with a possibility of 30–40 new members.

Always run tests on things like this and monitor it. If only 10 people join out of 200 vouchers is it worth it financially? Check the figures and assess this for your *own* marketplace.

I would reckon this kind of offer is usually worth a go because out of those 10 new members –

a) most stay and re-join
b) new members bring friends and family (for whom you will offer special vouchers of course!)

Add these facts to the equation and the real worth of the test will become evident.

Marketing with Punch's Golden Nuggets

Your existing customers are a goldmine and should be prospected frequently. New customers, although necessary are expensive to get. Do a great job and your existing customers will use you over and over again.

Groups of retailers

You may be a part of a secondary row of shops or high street precinct of retailers where you all want to encourage more people to the area. This benefits you all, right?

Work out a scheme that gives a 10% voucher or loyalty card for the participating shops in that group and ensure these go out with the local papers or leaflet distributors. The shared costs on the scheme mean it will cost each retailer a minimum amount.

A differing approach could be to produce a sheet that details special offers/B.O.G.O.Fs* or freebies that each individual store offers. This can increase numbers dramatically. You can put this in a local newspaper for distribution or have it delivered individually.

Attempt to put a perceived value on each offer (eg. a free dooberry dangle worth £5.85 with every bag of scrappies dog food) and put a cut off time to encourage immediate action.

Maintenance/cleaning services

Your services may include maintaining electrical goods, boilers, cars or valets, so decide whether the following brilliant idea could work for you.

Each time you go to a job give out a £X voucher with the clients name on. These can be given to family or friends to use against your service. The

---

*B.O.G.O.F. is a "buy one, get one free" offer.

client enjoys giving their family or friends this 'valuable' voucher, so referral is almost guaranteed!

When these new prospects use your service, you send the referral source a voucher by way of thanking them for referring you.

This encourages referrals *greatly*, keeps them using *you* and if they refer enough people, their next service call costs them nothing! You make your customer a no-wage salesperson! This can be used in all sorts of service industries with brilliant effect.

Upper-end business

By 'upper-end' we mean businesses that generate high spend/high profit. Everyone loves a free holiday, so offer a decent one to clients who refer you X amount of customers. (This need not be customers only, but may include allied trades or professions.)

Mail this to your old clients and colleagues and watch what happens. Bearing in mind the holiday may cost £2000 or more, ensure the financial outlay is worth this investment!

This can also be effectively done on the lower end of the profit scales. Your market may be youngsters whose ideal holiday is a piss-up and shagfest to the latest trendy country which *you* can buy quite cheaply.

Most important in this case is to accurately gauge the type of client you are aiming at and level the offer to their tastes. This is reasonably straight forward.

If you are selling £100,000 cars, you wouldn't offer the "knees up in Majorca", would you?! Likewise, if you sell rip-off designer gear in Romford, a two week health spa break would be as welcome as itching powder in your "snide" Calvin Klein's! Think before you do offers and consider the class structure of the likely recipients.

I love this 'high-end' idea!

Your client has just spent a large sum on a holiday or piece of jewellery, etc with your company. Send a bouquet to their office. Everyone is so bloody nosey that they immediately want to know who it is from. What a great company that takes the trouble to send a bouquet?

Warning – ensure that the item has not been bought for 'another' woman or man other than the husband or wife or fireworks may explode in your face.

Marketing with Punch's Golden Nuggets
Whenever preparing written copy, explain *exactly* and in simple terms what you do. We live in a very 'dumbed down' culture, and peoples lack of IQ will astound you!

Front-end referral

This is referral in its simplest form, and is quite widely used in seminars, theatres, concerts, etc.

Group booking discounts literally get your customers selling seats for you!

For example if the ticket price is £100, you could do 2 people at £89 each, 3–5 for £78 each, and six and above for £70 each; numbers over 10 are £65 each and one person (your salesperson!) gets a freebie!

A simple idea for getting bums on seats.

Marketing with Punch's Golden Nuggets
when a customer passes compliment on your product or service then is the time to pounce and ask for referrals or testimonials. This catches the person 'fresh' with enthusiasm for your product or service!

The 'free' facial

Have you noticed how make-up counters in department stores are always offering free facials or skin analysis?

What is the general reason for this? Simply that the client loves the result, buys all the make-up used, and continues to do so!

Is there a way your business could utilise this method in some way?

Always be on the lookout for ideas to hijack from other *types* of businesses, and adapt them to *your* use.

Marketing with Punch's Golden Nuggets
When writing copy, focus on your
customer's problems or wants and not
your product!

The emotional 'clincher'

A clever system very 'casually' used by a pet shop owner is one that really made me laugh for its ingenuity!

I suppose the same thing is used by car dealers on 'weekend loans' of desirable cars.

The crux of it was that if a suitable couple was hesitant about buying a particular puppy or kitten he would let them take it home for the weekend (with today's credit/debit card system it was easy to take the money then refund it *if* the person returned).

You've probably guessed the rest . . . Would the family let the puppy be returned to the shop? You bet 99 times out of a hundred a huge "NO"! The family had fallen in love with it.

Do you have a product where you could 'lend' it for a specified period (or at least a sample version you keep in stock)?

You literally want the customer to fall in love with your product!

Send out case histories of happy customers

Write case histories where your customers have loved what you have done for them, and do a regular mailing to prospects who have not yet acted.

These can be on high quality photocopies (or printed by a commercial printer) enclosed in a neat folder.

On each A4 sheet do a separate story of how you really knocked a customer's socks off, preferably with a picture of the happy customer with quotes.

Do *not* make these stories about how *great* your company is, but what you have done for the lucky customer and how their life is now better.

For example, start the story with how great Mrs Green's new conservatory is and how much more room she has in her house. Then add how pleased she was with the professional service, price, and excellent quality of product and workmanship.

What is in the deal for the potential customer is the all important clincher.

We Sell, We Don't 'Show Off'

You may ask when do we show off? Big companies do it, don't they?

Big companies advertising is done by advertising agencies whose main aim is to 'brand build' not sell *directly*, as smaller companies have to.

The advertising does not really have to quantify by way of direct sales/calls from that ad, but slowly and cleverly build/hold their name in the market.

Unless you own McDonalds, IBM or Coca-Cola, your ads have to pay or you will go broke! Simple!

To become a major brand takes time, and if you look at the early history of these brands their advertising was 'selling based' far more so than they now need to be. (Read the history of, for example, Coca-Cola).

There are big brands that simply cannot sell what they do and have to rely on branding and image creation only. Imagine truthfully selling *some* products on what they actually *do*. For example:

SNOW DUCKS VODKA
"gets you pissed real quick!"

BURTON & REGIS CIGARETTES
"make you smell, gets you hooked and eventually kills you"
— WOW!

You see why some companies can *only* brand-build? If they do not have 'benefits' to sell, an *image* must be created.

Free 'Screening'

Why not use a free screening service for your industry?

This has been successfully used by one of our consultants, an osteopath.

When new patients come in he waits until they are beginning to feel a lot better then he asks if any of the family or friends have back or neck problems. He then writes a voucher with the patients name, and expiry date.

The voucher explains that this is strictly for close friends or family of "Mr Smith" and that they are entitled to a 'free screening'.

The voucher explains that this is offered by the clinic as a 'thank you' to the above named patient.

This works wonders for his practice but could also work in many other businesses where checking a job beforehand (estimate or quote?) can be 'sexed up' into the more exclusive sounding 'free screening'.

Brainstorm how *your* business sector could do this.

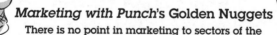

Marketing with Punch's Golden Nuggets
There is no point in marketing to sectors of the market unable to afford your product or service. E.g. would you offer an expensive book or course on "How To Overcome Bankruptcy"? Make sure your chosen market can *afford* what you do.

Info Booklets

Let us look a little closer than we did in the earlier chapter, at information booklets.

There is some great mileage in this brilliant and fairly low cost piece of marketing.

Information booklets should be short and sweet, 6 pages as an example, and no bigger than A5.

How do these differ from a brochure? Simply they are a 'consumer advice' package with an *undercurrent* of selling.

For example – What do you want from a 4x4 car?

You may sell used 4x4 cars or be a main dealer for one make. With the former you literally need to offer information on the different makes and models of 4x4 and what each offers so that the customer understands which model is best at what role.

With the latter you do the same thing except introduce your full range with inherent advantages of each one. Use these information booklets to *educate* without too much bias. You *only* introduce your company in the last part of the info booklet.

When introducing yourselves you must avoid the "corporate march" and tell the customer why using you is easier and preferable.

For example: How would you like a totally unbiased opinion on which 4x4 is best for your needs?

At Hunter-Bloggs 4x4 we are not biased to any one brand and can tailor a car for *you*.

Our team are all genuine 4x4 enthusiasts and over the years our customers return again and again.

You get to benefit from all this unbiased expertise, and how about this amazing deal?

If you do not like the 4x4 we sell you, bring it back in 3 days and exchange it for a different model! Wow!

(Make this subject to conditions which you will need a relevant lawyer to help you draw up).

Furthermore, we offer very tempting part exchange and finance deals.

See the pattern? Your copy is full of how you help the customer and not how great Hunter-Bloggs 4x4 are, what lovely corporate colours they have, and who the manager is. No one gives a flying f*** about *that*!

You can use these info booklets in almost *any* business, and worded correctly they can influence potential buyers greatly.

A 'mistakes' section is great. No one likes to make a cock-up when choosing a product or service.

Try a 'take' on these

- the 7 mistakes people make when choosing new windows
- common mistakes people make when writing a will
- will you make these mistakes when choosing a hotel for corporate clients?
- easy mistakes to make when choosing a cookery course

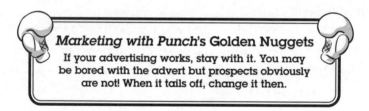

Marketing with Punch's Golden Nuggets
If your advertising works, stay with it. You may be bored with the advert but prospects obviously are not! When it tails off, change it then.

The 4x4 car example is in all probability not your industry, but can you see how this works in almost any industry, and can help to flatten your competitor's dull unhelpful image?

I saw a lovely booklet aimed at a printer's customers which was entitled "It's Never Too Early For a Reprint" which literally, by thoughtful wording, told businesses not to run out of their printed goods and order more – *Now*!

If the title of the booklet is well thought out as this one was, even if the person did not read the booklet, the title alone got them thinking (and buying). Our *title* is our headline. Our headline gets *ATTENTION*.

Examples could be

Garage door installer –
"Well functioning garage doors are a rare luxury. We make it happen".

Heating engineer –
"Well installed heating is a luxury few homes *really* enjoy . . . Now you can benefit from this".

Website designer –
"When your website simply has to bring results, we *make* it happen".

Hairdresser –
"Most stylists merely cut hair . . . we *create* styles!"

or

"go to an 'everyday' hair stylist for an everyday cut. When you simply *have* to look your best, we are here for you!"
Note: Very powerful message. When would a woman not want to look her best?

Can you see how these titles entice readership and action?

Would a back pain sufferer open a booklet that said . . .

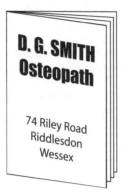

Or would they be more likely to open a booklet that reads:

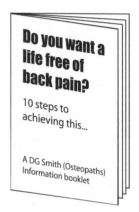

See the difference? You have appealed to your prospects wants and needs.

Take the time to sit and write at least 100 headlines and pick a few you love.

Test these in small print-runs to see which pulls in the most response before you go gung-ho into getting 3 million booklets done. Or . . . If you have 3 headlines with 'wow' factor, get a third of the booklets done with each one; suck it and see how people respond. *Then* you can proceed to X thousand copies with greater confidence. *And* make sure your booklets contain information that really helps the reader *besides* your own professional services. Always offer a helpful slant that gives advice which does not directly need your services.

Marketing with Punch's Golden Nuggets

People fear loss more than they value gain.
Point out how much your product can save them.
Look at how many cars are sold on their 'low fuel costs' and low car tax brackets. People will go to more effort to protect what they have rather than go to the effort of *gaining*.

Websites And Brochures

The lifeblood of many successful companies, apart from advertising, is how effective their website and brochure is.

There are very few enterprises where a brochure is not a necessity, and a website is a *must* nowadays for 99% of companies as prospects want information on your business quickly. If they can't access *your* information, they will soon access your *competitor's* information!

A website or brochure needs to be fed by advertising campaigns, or, apart from search engines where you are amongst many others, no-one will find you. Being top of the list on search engines is all very well, and probably vital, but a business that wants to grow rapidly needs more means than Google alone to push traffic to their site. In the general run of business, those that wish to grow profits and market share use more than just the internet; (remember, even eBay and Friends Reunited advertise on television and in the media!)

Consider general marketing and advertising as a means of creating interest in your goods. Your brochure and website should 80% 'pre-sell' the customer to you then your brilliantly trained sales people should seal the deal.

Some businesses, particularly those starting on a smaller scale, will use leaflets rather than brochures, but the same copy writing principles apply.

The website or brochure must markedly point out to the customer what is in it for them, so do not merely concentrate on making a flashy website without great marketing tools.

Make the site easy to navigate as not everyone is brilliant with computers. This ensures people of lower computer literacy can use your information with ease.

Avoid pictures of your shop, office and general tittle-tattle on how great you are (let scattered 'testimonials' do this job for you). Pictures of your premises, (unless very relevant) tell people nothing.

A brochure or website is designed to attract customers, not win the boardroom's approval!

An institutional type brochure is ok for companies of high (and well known) prestige. Examples could be:-

- Bentley
- Rolls-Royce
- Holland & Holland
- Armani

Most of the customers obtaining these brochures pretty much know what they want. These companies can afford to be 'company boastful' as their general image is already well known, and a lot of their marketing can afford to be brand building.

However, even these great names have competition, so a certain amount of selling is still required to inform customers of the USPs. Even these companies have competition to an extent!

- Bentley/Rolls Royce are competing with e.g. Maybach or Mercedes S Class
- Holland & Holland compete with Purdey or Boss
- Armani have to compete with other luxury brands of which there are now many

But it still remains true that much of their marketing can safely and effectively be brand and image building (although this image building needs backing up with good 'sales driven' copy writing to differentiate benefits from competitors.

Our own brochure and website required us to dilute specialist knowledge into an easy to understand version which addressed prospects needs. Would your product need this approach making it easier to understand for your clients? Let a total lay-person read it and check it is completely understandable.

What this requires is a way to explain "Micron assisted diddly widgets" in a way that meets only what your customers' needs are. The technical stuff can wait until the end of the brochure as there undoubtedly is a sector who will relish this information.

Add relevant pictures to this brochure and you will appeal to all the prospects' senses.

Visual – pictures
Auditory – words
Kinaesthetic – they 'feel' the need for the product

Prospects will function strongest on one or two of the above levels so we broaden our client scope, using these factors alone.

Make sure all photos are relevant, and if you put in mug shots of staff, realise this is only for familiarisation, and if space is a premium, is not a major selling tool.

However, if the photos are relevant, and you can use the staff pictures to add information on what you *do* for the customer, by all means produce a 'meet the staff' page. You may also consider this section to emphasise company size.

Some companies have a wide scope of client and need different brochures to cater for differing levels of intelligence or class.

To get over this we may have to produce a number of different websites or brochures to appeal to, for example, in what level of media we advertise?

If you advertise in a low-end tabloid, and in the high-brow newspapers such as *The Times* or *Telegraph* it is obvious the respondents will differ greatly and your copy must cater for this client differentation.

Or you may find that there is more than one *use* for the same product or service depending on who will use it. For example a battery powered camping light could also be used in a greenhouse where there is no mains electric. How many uses does your product or service have?

> ### *Marketing with Punch's* Golden Nuggets
> *Value your product*
> When your dentist pulls out a tooth and charges you £400, you are not buying 2 minutes of work, you are buying value. It did not take him two minutes to learn, it took him many years of training. People buy perceived value, not material cost.

A guide to brochure layout

Don't ever send out a brochure without a sales letter attached to the front.

As an example, this is what we send with one of our company's brochures.

REGISTERED OSTEOPATHS
SPECIALIST ORTHOTIC PRESCRIPTION SERVICE

46 Banstead Road Carshalton Beeches Surrey SM5 3NW   Telephone & Facsimile: 020 8404 6860

Dear Sir/Madam

Thank you for taking the time to contact us for our clinic information pack.

Suffering from foot or heel pain as you very likely do, we are sure you will find our 98.95% success rate very encouraging and our 100% money back guarantee a strong reason to make the journey to see us.

As the most successful foot and heel pain specialists outside the USA, and with only one visit usually being necessary, we are very sure we will be welcoming you to our clinic soon.

In the unlikely event of you not wishing to book your free consultation with us immediately, why not order a copy of **"The Layman's Guide To Foot And Heel Pain"** written by our Senior Biomechanics Consultant. It is incredibly easy to read and full of useful information.

Should you have any queries after reading this pack or wish to take advantage of our free consultation please do not hesitate to contact a member of our advisory team on **020 8404 6860.**

Yours sincerely

L Bailey and S Williams
Company Directors

www. heelspur.co.uk
A Division of Parish & Bell LTD
Company registration No: 4906208

Parish & Bell Clinic's introductory letter is attached to every brochure

This introduces your company and brochure content, and has a nice pre-sales touch to it.

Introduce what you do, why you lead your field, and why the enclosed brochure holds the answers to your customers problems.

When you sign off, get your printer to print the signatures so they look like they have been hand written in *blue* ink. This is *very* effective.

Finally, for most companies you must add a 'ps' (you will notice our own letter does not have a ps, as it's not really appropriate for a medical company!!). This is more widely read than the rest of the letter so should contain your most powerful message. However, make sure a p.s is relevant to your image.

Brochure front cover

You may use the term 'brochure' or 'widget consumer guide', it's up to you to decide the 'pitch' of your company. *Consumer guide* will generally lead more people toward its helpful nature.

Use a good quality picture that captures the 'essence' of what you provide (*don't* use a picture of your office or shop!). **Add your website address and phone number** *on every page* **including the cover**.

Of course you need to put your company name on the front if only to identify to whom the brochure refers!

Let's look at possible layout

1st page A personal message from the directors
Use this to introduce your service and describe how your goals are to solve your customers' needs. Don't use it to waffle about yourselves.

2nd page A page of testimonials
Let your past customers tell your prospects how great you are. This can also be the page where you direct people to the '80 amazing customer stories' that are in full on your website!

Page 3 What makes us so special when you the customer, has so much choice?
Identify and show off your USP's[1] to full effect and unashamedly. This stands you out from the crowd, and gives customers a reason to choose your company.

Page 4 Your unique approach
Sell how you do things better and why it solves their problem more effectively.

Page 5 What is a widget?
Explain exactly what the product is (you can use a *bit* of technical stuff at this stage if relevant and in *layman's* terms.) You are not trying to be technically clever here, you are *selling* why you and your product are so good.

Page 6 The technical blurb
Don't make a big song and dance with this, but you may need to appeal to the 'academic buyers' who want or need to know all the scientific data. This is primarily selling to a different type of person but also gives an 'edge' to non-academic buyers who will 'skim' this section but still be impressed by its mere presence.

Middle pages
If possible, utilise these to reproduce any press/media clippings on your company or business; or you may find press cuttings that talk about your industry, casting your particular type of company or association membership in a favourable light? This approach is credibility building at its easiest.

Further pages may include
- Other types of widget available. Talk about their weaknesses compared to yours (without mentioning competitor's names or trademarks!)
- State your guarantees and how these are put into action. Boast how your company is so confident it only seemed logical to offer the guarantee

---

[1]Chapter 3 – (Unique Selling Points) and Niche Markets

- You may wish to point out other services your company offers if relevant
- Obviously, right from the opening page you will want to offer your book for sale. Immediately this puts you on an author/expert pedestal in the customers mind. (Don't forget to include an easy to use order form or website link so they can order it!)
- List all/any professional associations or awards your company has got or earned
- Add a '10 mistakes people make when buying widgets' and a '10 advantages of *using your company*' section
- You will want an easy to understand step by step guide on how to use your company. When on an internet site, make every step *easy* to get to checkout or order, and, as I repeat, make it easy to contact your business

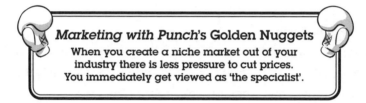

Marketing with Punch's Golden Nuggets
When you create a niche market out of your
industry there is less pressure to cut prices.
You immediately get viewed as 'the specialist'.

- Make sure that in at least two places in the brochure there is a contact section. This must include phone, website, information line, fax, email enquires and, if relevant, out of hours numbers. **Out of hours** can mean the difference in you or a competitor getting the order!
- A favourite ending to any website or brochure is a 'commonly asked questions' section.

Between yourself and your staff spend time thinking about what are the most common questions asked by prospects on the phone or face to face.

Having these in your brochure/website can save a lot of time on the phone or in face to face selling situations.

Other ideas for you to think about

- A map/public transport details of your location
- Free sample
- Money off voucher
- Free consultation
- 2 for 1 offer
- A password to 'special customers' allowing access to an exclusive area of your website
- A bonus to act within days/weeks
- And very importantly – CAPTION EVERY PHOTOGRAPH
  A picture means nothing without an explanation!
- If you produce a company magazine or information booklets, have these available to download or read on your website
- A downloadable version of your book?
- An online video presentation?
- Make your brochure downloadable/printable from your website. This costs you nothing and can save a lot on postage

In other words – optimise your site or brochure. You simply cannot oversell!!

Internet Marketing

Much is written about Internet marketing by some very able experts who work purely in this field, and we implore our readers to investigate these many learned avenues.

Our opinion is that Internet Marketing should be a *part* of what you do to increase sales.

We all look for specific items on the internet for ease of sourcing, with a few exceptions. But if you want to grow *really* big, people must be *guided* to your site by way of general media advertising.

Whilst it's true that many people do make a great living from the internet, we do want a lot *more* sales and growth, don't we? We do not want to merely 'make a living', we want to build a business.

Even the giants of the internet such as 'eBay' and 'Friends Reunited', in themselves brilliantly conceived sites, advertise heavily on the television and in the press. This alerts the sectors of the market who do not 'trawl' the internet and need telling that the site is there.

We could call this 'brand awareness' but to simplify this look on it as a 'nudge and reminder', for doesn't everyone know eBay and Friends Reunited? There are always sectors in the marketplace that need reminding you are there and what you can offer them.

Our own business is kept near to the top of the search engines by professionals in this field, and although this is not a cheap option, it keeps us there in the internet public's eye.

It may also be prudent to employ a person to solely carry out your email mail shots for you, perhaps once every four weeks?

As already stated, there are a few exceptions that can stay solely on the internet, but these are very few. Even suppliers of specialist sports equipment or the like also advertise in specialist magazines.

What if you have a product that people don't know they want? For example, a limited edition plate featuring cats in Father Christmas outfits? You would generally advertise this in a magazine but may also have this on eBay under 'cats', or even use your magazine advert to direct people to your website where there may be other equally tasteless items!! The magazine advert will also offer non internet users an easy way to order a specific product. Remember that many customers do not even have internet access.

Always expand your thinking into as many marketing directions as you can, and keep testing!

An interesting story of brochures versus website . . .

When our company suffered a flood in our basement storage area, we had to wait two weeks to get more brochures printed as these were destroyed in the flooding. All the information was there on the website for people to read, but our customer numbers fell dramatically until the brochures were sent! My feeling on this is that people still trust a 'tangible' brochure more than a website. Or, was it that a brochure is easier to pick-up and read at leisure? Either way, let this be food for thought.

Advertising And Copy Writing

The amount of people we speak to who proudly boast, "I have never advertised and look at us". People who own needlessly un-ambitious small companies usually utter this. Cleverly targeted advertising will make your profits soar *if done correctly*.

Where and how to advertise have always been a major headache to the entrepreneur.

The secret is to target your advertising to the type of customer you want or need.

Returning, as an example, to the 'plate featuring cats in Father Christmas outfits'; we would not advertise this in high-brow newspapers such as *The Times* or *Daily Telegraph*.

Likewise we would not advertise an academic product or service in *The Daily Sport* or *Daily Star*.

We would also avoid specialist products in non-specialist publications as we are aiming at a small 'core sector' or niche market.

Specialist magazines where we may sell certain sporting items or items aimed at, for example, certain car enthusiasts, specialist railway fans, dog breeders, etc, will generally advertise exactly what they offer and perhaps lead people to a website or brochure that gives them more choice of product from the company.

Newspapers and 'general topic' magazines are an expensive option, but media we need to be in if hitting a non-specific audience where almost anyone may need or want our product.

We must ensure that the newspaper of choice attracts the right type of reader for our product.

Every country has its own newspapers written for their chosen market sector, and it should not be difficult to work this out for your own country's media by looking at the UK examples below.

- *The Daily Mirror* predominantly older generation working-class people, although it does now also enjoy a younger sector
- *The Sun* – mixed age, working and lower middle class. A huge circulation which also encompasses all classes of people looking for a 'light-read'.
- *The Times* – upper middle class, entrepreneurs, lawyers and professionals
- *The Daily Mail* – middle class England! Great circulation of quality customers generally 35+ in age
- *The Telegraph* – middle class, generally fairly academic. A little 'staid', but this is its appeal.
- *The Guardian* – educated readership, teachers, social workers, university graduates
- *The Daily Sport* and *Daily Star* – Soft porn and sport readership. Very light and 'fun' reading.

All of these are very successful newspapers who know their audience well, and before embarking on advertising with any newspaper, get to know your prospects lifestyles, needs, wants and passions.

It goes without saying that local newspapers can be a lifeline for local businesses. You need to really stand out in these as hundreds of other businesses will be competing head to head with you, so really learn the art of advertising before you put in any old poorly written advertisement.

We love testimonial type advertising where a true story of a past customer is used as the basis of the advert copy. Remember how powerful it is when a *customer* says how great you are?

'40 Years of Heel Pain - GONE!'

David Wilkinson

AFTER 40 years of agonising foot pain David Wilkinson finally found the answer to his prayers!

Since childhood David Wilkinson had suffered from painful feet. But now it had become so uncomfortable he could barely walk to the bathroom in the morning and every day he longed for relief from the searing pain in his heels.

David, 64, from Hampshire, was suffering from Plantar Fasciitis, a condition where the ligament type structures that support the arch of the foot start to inflame and small tears can occur throughout these ligaments, causing excruciating pain in the heel and/or arch of the foot.

98.95% success rate

He went to his GP who prescribed anti inflammatories and cortisone injections, but neither gave any real relief. In the following years David tried all kinds of treatments including physiotherapy, podiatry and a range of foot pads, but again to no avail.

'Everybody seemed to have a name for the pain I was getting but I couldn't work out why nobody could help me!' says David. 'This went on for years as I went in and out of surgeries, trying every method of self-help available.' In 1990 his condition started to deteriorate and in 1997 he was told he would need an operation to release the 'plantar ligament' underneath each foot. 'It sounded drastic to have an operation, but I was now in agony. I had to go ahead with it,' explains David.

Sadly, neither operation was a success and recovery was long and painful. 'I was shattered to find it had not worked,' says David. The pain was worsening daily and walking was becoming unbearable.'

Years passed and in 1999 David retired on medical grounds. 'I was in disbelief, how could the pain have got so bad that it ended my career and worse still, how come no-one could help me? I wasn't suffering from a rare illness, it was heel pain!'

Free consultation

After various other failed attempts to find help over the next five years David was reading the paper when he noticed an advert offering 100 per cent guaranteed relief from heel pain. 'I didn't take a lot of notice,' explained David. 'It was just another gimmick, I had heard it all before,' he remembers.

David saw the article several times. Eventually he called the number and requested an information pack. He read it with interest—these people actually sounded as if they could help. The clinic used a 3D laser scanner which measures the foot 64,000 times every inch and produces orthotics to an accuracy of 1/10,000th of an inch.

The clinic was located south of London. David was shocked, it seemed a long way to travel. But then he noticed that only one visit was usually necessary and so the clinic actually

One visit: The 3D optical laser scanner at the Parish & Bell

helped patients from all over the world.

David took the plunge and booked an appointment. What were a few hours of travelling after decades of pain?

He arrived at the clinic for an assessment and was impressed. The staff were attentive, experienced and completely understood his pain. Their knowledge of heel pain amazed me,' he explained. 'Sadly, however, my story was not unique to them. In fact, it was more of a common occurrence. I decided to proceed with the orthotics—it was guaranteed to work, after all.'

Les Bailey, Senior Biomechanics Consultant at the Parish & Bell Clinic and author of The Layman's Guide To Foot And Heel Pain, explains: 'I suffered from Plantar Fasciitis myself in my 20s and found no help. I was an osteopath back then and was amazed at the lack of help or knowledge of the condition.

Painless procedure

'This sent me on a mission to find relief and I was introduced to the 3D optical foot laser from America. This laser is now one weapon in our armoury. But it's our unique specialisation and experience in treating heel pain that allows us to achieve such dramatic results with patients who have suffered for decades. This enables us to give a 100 per cent money back guarantee* to clear up the pain.'

After 17 years of dealing with foot and heel pain, the clinic now receives patients from all over the globe and has an astonishing 98.95 per cent success rate.

Three weeks later David's orthotics arrived and within a few days he was pain free.

One Visit

'I couldn't believe it and still can't,' he exclaims. 'Forty years of suffering and it was banished in one visit. It's like a miracle for me. It has completely changed my life.'

The clinic also treats many other foot complaints including pain in the ball of the foot, ankle pain, Mortons Neuroma and shin splints.

Patient David Wilkinson: 'It's like a miracle and has changed my life'

Specialist models of orthotics including sports, golf, hiking, slim fits and many more can also be prescribed by the clinic.

For a FREE information pack, more advice or to book an appointment contact Parish & Bell Clinic on the main telephone number. 020 8404 6860. If all their advisers are busy when telephoning the clinic please leave a message and your call will be returned as quickly as possible. Alternatively write to 46 Banstead Road, Carshalton, Surrey SM5 3NW. www.parishandbell.co.uk

Out of hours recorded information line 'Learn about your foot or heel pain' 020 8395 3551 (Not a premium rate number)

* Subject to patients attending four free adjustment visits.
© Parish and Bell Ltd 2006

As Featured in National Press and Radio

A VERY *Special Offer* to those with Foot or Heel Pain

This book has greatly helped thousands just like you to regain their active lives. Foot pain is a misery you don't have to live with.

The incredible success of "The Layman's Guide to Foot and Heel Pain" means we are producing new editions constantly. Already the best selling book in its category, we now feel it's time to give something back to the community, so we are donating £1 from every book sold to childrens mobility charities.

Not only are we donating £1 to childrens charity, but we are **Enclosing a FREE DVD** to accompany the book.

Written by Les Bailey, Senior Consultant at the famous Parish & Bell Clinic, the book simplifies for the lay person how to help long standing foot or heel problems. With a wealth of many years experience, Les's book will ease you through the complex minefield of foot pain interestingly and easily.

What people just like you have said:
"I would never have thought someone could make foot pain such an interesting read" D.G

"Your book literally saved me. Thank you so much" A.N

The Layman's Guide to FOOT and HEEL PAIN
A guide to the unbreakable laws of curing foot and heel pain

HEEL PAIN WEBSITE UPDATED
Read 80 new amazing testimonials today www.heelspur.co.uk

To Order by Debit or Credit Card Phone

020 8404 6860

or send a cheque or postal order to Parish & Bell Ltd, 46 Banstead Road, Carshalton, Surrey SM5 3NW

Special Offer Just £3.77 + 70p P&P STRICTLY LIMITED OFFER ACT NOW!
Usual Price £9.95 + Postage

www.heelspur.co.uk

This is an example of a favourite advert that we produced for our clinic, and which we have used for a long time. We will point out the areas we used and why we used them.

Notice the general copy wording? See how it leads the reader from sentence to sentence, giving lots of relevant information. Wouldn't you be irresistibly drawn to that advert if *you* had heel pain?

'40 Years of Heel Pain - GONE!'

David Wilkinson

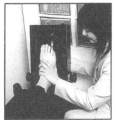

Patient David Wilkinson: 'It's like a miracle and has changed my life'

AFTER 40 years of agonising foot pain David Wilkinson finally found the answer to his prayers!

Since childhood David Wilkinson had suffered from painful feet. But now it had become so uncomfortable he could barely walk to the bathroom in the morning and every day he longed for relief from the searing pain in his heels.

David, 64, from Hampshire, was suffering from Plantar Fasciitis, a condition where the ligament type structures _____ _____port the arch of the foot start to ____ _d small tears can occur through_____ ___aments, causing excruciating pain _____ el and/or arch of the foot.

98.95% success rate

He went to his GP who prescribed anti inflammatory and cortisone injections, but neither gave any real relief. In the following years David tried all kinds of treatments including physiotherapy, podiatry and a range of foot pads, but again to no avail.

'Everybody seemed to have a name for the pain I was getting but I couldn't work out why nobody could help me!' says David. 'This went on for years as I went in and out of surgeries, trying every method of self-help available.' In 1990 his condition started to deteriorate and in 1987 he was told he would need an operation to release the 'plantar ligament' underneath each foot. 'It sounded drastic to have an operation, but I was now in agony. I had to go ahead with it,' explains David.

Sadly, neither operation was a success and recovery was long and painful. 'I was shattered to find it had not worked,' says David. The pain was worsening daily and walking was becoming unbearable.'

Years passed and in 1999 David retired on medical grounds. 'I was in disbelief, how could the pain have got so bad that ___ded my career and worse still, how c___ could help me? I wasn't sufferin___ ___ illness, it was heel pain!'

Free consultation

After various other failed attempts to find help over the next five years David was reading the paper when he noticed an advert offering 100 per cent guaranteed relief from heel pain. 'I didn't take a lot of notice,' explained David. 'It was just another gimmick, I had heard it all before,' he remembers.

David saw the article several times. Eventually he called the number and requested an information pack. He read it with interest — these people actually sounded as if they could help. The clinic used a 3D laser scanner which measures the foot 64,000 times every inch and produces orthotics to an accuracy of 1/10,000th of an inch.

The clinic was located south of London. David was shocked, it seemed a long way to travel. But then he noticed that only one visit was usually necessary and so the clinic actually

One visit: The 3D optical laser scanner at the Parish & Bell

helped patients from all over the world.

David took the plunge and booked an appointment. What were a few hours of travelling after decades of pain?

He arrived at the clinic for an assessment and was impressed. The staff were attentive, experienced and completely understood his pain. 'Their knowledge of heel pain amazed me,' he explained. 'Sadly, however, my story was not unique to them. In fact, it was more of a common occurrence. I decided to proceed with the orthotics — it was guaranteed to work, after all.'

Les Bailey, Senior Biomechanics Consultant at the Parish & Bell Clinic and author of The Layman's Guide To Foot And Heel Pain, explains: 'I suffered from Plantar Fasciitis myself in my 20s and ___ help. I was an osteopath back th___ amazed at the lack of help or h___ the condition.'

Painless procedure

'This sent me on a mission to find relief and I was introduced to the 3D optical foot laser from America. This laser is now one weapon in our armoury. But it's our unique specialisation and experience in treating heel pain that allows us to achieve such dramatic results with patients who have suffered for decades. This enables us to give a 100 per cent money back guarantee* to clear up the pain.'

After 17 years of dealing with foot and heel pain, the clinic now receives patients from all over the globe and has an astonish___ __.95 per cent success rate.

Three weeks later David's ortho_____ and within a few days he was pai___

One Visit

'I couldn't believe it and still can't,' he exclaims. 'Forty years of suffering and it was banished in one visit. It's like a miracle for me. It has completely changed my life.'

The clinic also treats many other foot complaints including pain in the ball of the foot, ankle pain, Mortons Neuroma and shin splints.

Specialist models of orthotics including sports, golf, hiking, slim fits and many more can also be prescribed by the clinic.

For a FREE information pack ___ ___ice or to book an appointment c___ __ & Bell Clinic on the main telep___ ___ber. 020 8404 6860. If all their advi___ ___busy when telephoning the clinic please leave a

mes_____ ___ur call will be re___ quick___ __ible. Alternative___ 46 Banstead Road, Carshalton, S___ 3NW. www.parishandbell.co.uk

Out of hours recorded information line 3551 (Not a premium rate number___

*Subject to patients attending four free adjus___
© Parish and Bell___

As Featured in National Pres___ ___adio

A VERY Special Offer to those with Foot or Heel Pain

This book has greatly helped thousands just like you to regain their activ___ Foot pain is a misery you don't live with.

The incredible success of 'The Layman's ___ to Foot and Heel Pain' means we are producing new editions constantly. Already the best selling book in its categor_____ ___ feel it's time to give something back ___ ___unity, so we are donating £1 fro____ ___old to childrens mobility chariti___

Not only are we do___ ___£1 to childrens charity, but we are **Enclosing a FREE DVD to accompany the book.**

Written by Les Bailey, Senior Consu____ famous Parish & Bell Clinic, the boo___ for the lay person how to help stop ___ foot or heel problems. With a wealth of many years experience, Les's book will ease you through the complex minefield of foot pain interestingly and easily.

What people just like you have said:
"I would never have thought someone could make foot pain such an interesting read" D.G

"Your book literally saved me. Thank you so much" A.N

The Layman's Guide to FOOT and HEEL PAIN — A guide to the unbreakable laws of curing foot and heel pain

LES BAILEY

HEEL PAIN WEBSITE UPDATED Read 80 new amazing testimonials today ___w.heelspur.co.uk

Special Offer Just £3.77 + 70p P&P

STRICTLY LIMITED OFFER ACT NOW!

To Order by Del___ ___Card ___me
020 84___ __360
or send a cheque ___ __ order to Parish & Bell Ltd, 46 Banstead Road, Carshalton, Surrey SM5 3NW

www.heelspur.co.uk

---

① Note – large interesting headline that will entice anyone with heel pain to read it! Note – headline mainly in *lower case* (easier to read).

② Photograph of the person the story is discussing. Adds 'gritty reality'.

③ Subheadings point out main features.

④ Notice how we do not make a huge song and dance of our name? We concentrate on the reader.

⑤ The entire advert looks like an 'article'.

⑥ A separate 'advert within an advert' looks like a normal newspaper page but 'attracts' by giving a separate 'take' on the whole page.

⑦ The special offer for the book entices more buyers. The book itself is a major marketing tool.

⑧ We include our recorded information line, adding that it is *not* a premium rate number.

⑨ The website is repeated twice.

⑩ The address is given for those preferring to 'write in'.

⑪ A strictly 'limited' offer entices instant action from the reader.

⑫ We make paying easy and point out we take credit/debit card or cheque/ postal order.

⑬ The advert is *copyrighted*!

⑭ The book has featured in national press and radio and we boast about this!!

⑮ Note how we guide people to 80 testimonials on our website (which are shown as 'full letters' just as we received them).

⑯ A free bonus DVD accompanies the book offer.

⑰ £1 from each order goes to charity. (Most people who enquire about the brochure also want a book.) Even making no real direct profit from the book, the amount made covers post, packing and brochure costs for mail-outs!

⑱ 'Sneak in' a few testimonials for the book.

⑲ Every picture needs a caption. Note, even the caption 'sells'!

Headline your advert!

When brainstorming headlines, avoid being smart by using funny wording. This depreciates from what you are marketing. By the same token, avoid puns; these are corny and sound like shit! The general feel a pun gives is one of tabloid journalism.

A headline that quotes someone and uses quotation marks is always a winner.

The headline must appeal to the reader's self-interest. Ask yourself what it is they are looking for, and then offer them the benefit you can give them.

Give the headline a 'newsy' feel to it, and where possible copy the publications font as far as the editor will allow.

> **_Marketing with Punch's_ Golden Nuggets**
> The job of marketing is purely to pre-sell a product. This makes the sales teams job so much easier and more effective. Marketers are the generals who plan a war! Salespeople are the soldiers who finish it!

Sell: avoid showing off corporate colours

Advertising must be salesmanship in print. Don't be scared of long copy – it is proven to sell products. If a person stops reading your copy halfway through, it is either:

- irrelevant waffle
- boring

Or, hopefully

- they have decided to already buy the product even before the copy is ended.

The latter is our aim (as if you didn't know that!)

Your great headline has already hooked the reader like a fish to a baited hook. Ask any fisherman and they will tell you the tough part now is landing the fish. This is the job of your copy!

Break up your copy with small sub-headings, and use these to point out your USPs.

Spend time on the headline

Write out at least 100 headlines and finally pick one that literally blows you away, and you know will really appeal to your customers wants and needs, and not your company's perceived 'bells and whistles'.

This is an exercise you can also do when you have a spare hour, e.g. on a train journey. Keep doing headlines even when you feel you have/or are using a great one.

Copy writing

The easiest way to write copy is to first list all the benefits you want to get over to readers about your product or service. This could be for example:

- 100% money back guarantee
- will never peel or flake
- 99.99% success rate
- lifetime guarantee
- will never shrink
- free consultation
- 5 years free servicing and parts!
- saves 20% fuel costs – every time
- never needs ironing
- goes much faster

And so on . . .

Don't miss any as you will want to use these as your sub-headings during the copy, where you can then expand on them during the copy itself.

Sub-headings will break up the text into easy to read portions for your prospect. In one huge 'blurb', the copy seems much more effort to read.

Wording that headline

Returning to headlines once more . . ..

A headline should scream something new, and exciting, and make the reader *want* to read more. The old tried and tested 'buzzwords' for headlines (and sub-headlines) are still as relevant as ever. We take no credit for any of these as they are etched in the 'sands of time' of advertising history.

Free

Revolutionary

Ultimate

Brilliant

Results

Easy way to . . .

Breakthrough

Amazing

New

Everything

Save

Secrets of . . .

Success

Now you can . . .

Announcing

At last . . .

How I . . .

Latest

Now . . .

Gone . . .

Putting it together

Returning to the '40 Years of Heel Pain Gone' advert; this was put together after many years of studying marketing.

Notice its 'framework' and how you can apply it to your own industry.

How big should my ad be?

Our own growth was attributed to how, where and what size space to advertise. Each time we increased our advert size the more response we got. Obviously this was also dependent on time of year or Public Holiday factors.

Our accountant went crazy at the proposed cost of the next jump in ad size, but taking the risk was our choice so we did it anyway!

Testing your advert

The strangest things happen in testing, and you have to think ahead of how and when to test an ad.

"When?" is a major factor, our first test on a full-page ad was tested in December. We realised it was the wrong time for our product, but impatience made us test anyway. Whilst it did not 'flop totally', the results weren't usable on a real test as our product is not the normal Xmas item! Beware and think ahead!

It has been said that the definition of insanity is doing the same thing over and over again and expecting a different result.

If an ad 'bombs' you either:

- have a crap product
- ad is in the wrong publication or place
- ad is poorly written
- in a bad part of the publication
- you offer no USPs[1] on a widely available product
- you could not 'back up' the ad by great response systems (e.g. your staff or phonelines.)
- too expensive on the product or service
- suspiciously cheap on product price
- ad is in at the wrong time of the year
- your headline did not *entice* the reader
- your copy was poorly written/uninteresting/boring
- you were amongst a 'cluster' of ads and did not 'stand out'

AIDA

"Aida" is a well-worn marketing phrase that is very relevant even in today's climate. What does it mean?

Attention. Interest. Decision. Action

---

[1]Chapter 3 – (Unique Selling Points) and Niche Markets

This is how your readers need to respond to an advert. At this stage in the book we really don't need to explain the whys and wherefores of AIDA!

Testimonials

Where relevant, always use testimonials in your adverts. These are very powerful indeed.

Give helpful advice

Include some helpful advice in your copy. Something that is not directly selling your product, but is helping the reader, is reckoned to net around 60–80% more response.

Don't be a comedian

Forget being a witty smart arse! Don't write adverts that use humour to sell. The best ads are those that inform the reader of something so they are pleasantly surprised and curious to try the product or service.

Every picture tells a story

Use photos in your ads to illustrate the product or service. A picture should not only tell a story, but should emphasise this within a caption. Try to never use photos without a caption. Avoid drawings in advertising. They do not illustrate nearly as well.

Our hero

We absolutely implore you to get your hands on everything written or recorded by 'Ted Nicholas'. He is the undisputed world champion of copy writing and advertising and look out for our own forthcoming title, *Advertising With Punch*.

'Magic words that grow your business' on audio is a great start, but do build a library of Ted's books and materials. He has sold billions of dollars worth of products using advertising.

Advertising is a major part of business, so utilise this amazing man's material, www.tednicholas.com.

Another great of advertising, although he leans toward larger companies, is David Ogilvy.

We have read and learned a lot from this man, so, as we said earlier in the book – read his approach. Ogilvy's books are available via Amazon, online.

Networking

Networking, as we know it in the UK, is generally used by 'Business to Business' marketers. In other words, any product or service another business can utilise.

There are groups, for example, that do early morning breakfast meets. These can be incredibly powerful as you get to know your customers personally before doing business.

It is useful if you are a 'social animal' and this type of person gets the most from these events. If that is not really you it may be prudent to send an employee or colleague who thrives on social interaction.

The ideal personality type is the sort of person who enjoys team sports and relishes mixing with all types of people (you all know the sort!). Entrepreneurs can often be quite insular people and prefer spending time at other aspects of business.

The advantage of networking is that it is very much like face to face selling where you build rapport quickly; with networking you have more time to build rapport over weeks or even months.

At these events you must be genuinely interested in the persons business to attract their interest to yours. This is an old selling technique, but it works a dream!

You may be called upon to literally network many times outside formal networking groups. Any time you meet a person and introduce your business you are literally 'networking'.

Always carry business cards at all times. That million dollar client may just happen to sit next to you in a restaurant! **Be prepared!**

Produce a Magazine or Newsletter

Here is a fact that will rock you into action to produce a magazine for your business.

Over 90% of people are more likely to read your magazine than your brochure!

And the beauty of this is . . .

You can say a whole lot more in a magazine than a brochure!

We live in a magazine or newsletter culture with thousands of titles out every month.

You can use a magazine or newsletter to tell success stories about your business, announce new launches and generally 'boast' more than you can in your brochure or website.

And another great advantage?

Most, all, or even more than the cost can be borne by other businesses of your demographic type buying *advertising* space in your magazine!

If budget is tight, get plenty of advertisers in its pages, which should pay for postage costs to post to clients as well as production costs.

A glossy magazine with the use of a professional designer, freelance photographer and print to 10,000 copies should cost in the region of £6,000.

A simple newsletter should cost a whole lot less, and if you can produce reasonable photos yourself, a great deal of cost will be saved. If you stick to black and white photos, the cost will be considerably less than a glossy magazine.

It is all too easy to think that your product or service does not warrant a magazine, or newsletter but consider how powerful this can be.

Remember, you are carving yourself into the *only* business customers want to use.

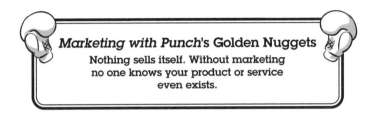

Marketing with Punch's Golden Nuggets

Nothing sells itself. Without marketing
no one knows your product or service
even exists.

Remember to sell the 'sizzle not the steak' within the magazines pages.

This means that if we sell building products, don't produce all the articles on certain bricks or window types, but skilfully show the finished interiors of homes built using your wares.

If you run singles' clubs, don't make articles all about dating, but show happy couple stories featuring past clients of yours.

You can showcase the far-reaching benefits of what you do in a magazine. Use this medium to the full.

Tips for magazine layouts

Cover – the cover should preferably show the face of a pretty girl! It has been proven with experimentation by editors of monthlies, that when pretty girls were substituted by products, magazine sales went down.

However, *enthusiast* titles such as railways, cars, pets, etc are an exception, so work out if your product really holds a 'passion' for the reader(?).

Index – have a proper index page much like any magazine.

Demographics – if your type of customer is upper middle class, base your magazine layout on an upmarket title like *Country Life*.

If your clientele are lower middle or working class, base the layout on a 'celebrity glossy' type magazine, easy to read and fun to flick through.

In short, we want our magazine read by our *type* of client, and if we aim too differently from this it stands less chance of being read.

Articles – whatever you do, make sure the articles are interesting to the *prospect*, not your colleagues. This means your staff may enjoy articles on the chemical make-up of your company's car tyres; your client will prefer an article on how fast your tyres allow him to take corners. Aim at your client; they are your buyers!

Generally speaking it is best to limit articles on your company's wares to 60%. The rest of the space goes to articles on other interesting topics. This keeps readers' interest.

You may have friends with businesses who would be only too glad to write an article of interest on their subject (or even hobbies?).

A great client who spends a fortune with you will really appreciate the opportunity to promote *their* business in your magazine, and this gives you a chance to say "thanks" for their custom in a creative and entrepreneurial way.

It should not be difficult to find people to write other articles of interest and to give breathing space from articles about your company.

Cover price – it is very important to give the magazine a perceived value. This makes it *worth reading* to its audience. A simple £2.30 *where sold* in the corner will suffice.

Scattered items – to break up the passages of text use crosswords, quizzes, a letters page, or even a celebrity quotes page.

You can even incorporate a jokes and/or 'weird facts' column appertaining to your product (these can usually be found on the internet!), these simply diffuse reams of text and make the whole body of the magazine more appealing to the eye.

Printing – magazine printing is rather specialised, and printers who do this can be found on the Internet.

Don't date your magazine – you want to do a second issue when it suits your timing. This may be one month or two years so do not 'date' articles, competitions or the cover.

Before printing, check *every* item for time-sensitivity so that it suits reprint times. Remember, you may plan a new magazine in three months time, but you may be way too busy for this, so don't let its contents dictate your schedule!

Parish & Bell magazine

Produce a Promotional DVD

A promotional DVD, when used correctly, can be a very powerful marketing adjunct.

Of all your promotional material a DVD can give a mighty clout to a campaign. Realistically it may only get played 40–70% of the time, so attempt to use it in circumstances it is certain to be played by your prospect.

We give our DVD as a 'free bonus' when people purchase 'The Layman's Guide to Foot and Heel Pain', so our prospects are far more likely to utilise it. You may find that you only send it out to select clients or those showing *real* interest in your product or service.

Do not ever home-make a DVD presentation using 'Bob from the pub's' borrowed DVD camera! When you produce a DVD, get it made properly by a professional company.

The cost should be around 2–3000 GBP, for a 15–20 minute production.

Individual DVDs can be replicated for around 0.35 GBP each.

Format

Like all our other material, our DVD must be designed to sell product or services and not merely fly our corporate colours for all to ignore.

Introduction – preferably by the director of the company. This must implant the message you want to give clearly, interestingly and explosively. In other words think 'a Tony Robbins presentation' and not a party political broadcast.

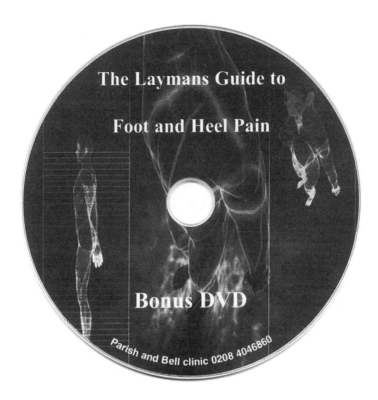

Like your brochure, the ethos must be toward your customers needs and wants and not your shareholders corporate expectations.

Testimonials – it's great when we get our champion customers who have been really pleased with what we have done for them, to appear on our DVD!

We found that no end of our happy customers were very willing to appear, and 99% were excellent on camera.

Make sure the testimonial is relevant to the structure of what you are imparting in your production and that the testimonials sell the actual product or service. To avoid the customer's nervousness on camera, our cameraman went to the clients own home and filmed them where they were more relaxed. Generally speaking, intersperse testimonials between other parts of the production.

Impart information

Give a section of useful information to the client that they can use to improve their lives. This takes the edge off the 'selling only' side.

Use other staff – you may have other staff whose specialities are usually marketed separately from the main run of the business, so use the DVD to introduce them.

You may wish to use parts of it to sell your book, other products you sell, or introduce future ideas for the business; but most importantly – **It must contain all your contact details during the DVD and also on its cover.**

Why?

Because the DVD can get separated from the brochure or book, or may be lent out on its own to prospects friends or family. If you notice we imprint our contact details onto the actual disk surface.

When selecting a company to produce your DVD, take time to look at their past work. The difference in quality can be truly amazing! We saw at least 4 people's work before choosing our DVD production company (see useful contacts section at the end of this book).

Sales Letters

Never send brochures or goods to a customer without an accompanying sales letter.

Your letter must be geared toward what you are sending out. If you are sending a brochure your letter must be full of passionate reinforcement of the product within in the brochure (see earlier chapter on brochures and websites).

Generally, a good sales letter has a headline – without this people won't read it.

Like all your advertising, the headline is the bait that catches the fish.

The headline must capture the essence of the presentation. It must outline the major benefit you are putting across. It must be credible and specific.

For example you may enjoy a 99.72% measured success rate in a business where success rates are notoriously low. Doesn't the extra work quantifying the 99.72%, instead of "over 99%" sound more credible?

A great headline can hook three times more people to read the copy than a poor headline.

The main body of the letter must be easy and interesting to read.

Use plenty of short sentences peppered with quality sub-headings (see earlier chapter on advertising). This will ensure reader digestibility.

Your sub-headings must preview what is about to be discussed, so think what would appeal to your wants and needs were *you* the customer.

Letters aimed at selling a product cannot, in essence, be too long, but they can easily be too boring; so keep the customer interested by avoiding useless diatribe. Ideally the person should want to buy when they are half way through the letter.

The feel of the letter must be about the prospect's needs coupled with why they should employ your company.

How do people read sales letters?

- they read the headline
- they quickly scan the sub-headings
- if it looks worth reading, they will read the "ps" first!

PSs

Certain sales letters warrant a good "ps" and even a "pps". Use this at the end to highlight a bonus offer or extra goody you are enticing them with.

Your ps is read as much as the headline so put a highly relevant point in it.

Always either hand sign your sales letter or get your printer to formulate your signature in a blue that replicates ink or biro. This adds clout to your letter (and *individuality*).

If numbers allow, hand write the envelope and stamp your letters. People are far more likely to open them this way. Don't *you* always open hand written envelopes first?

Stamp it

When people ask for your brochure or sales information it is very much more powerful to have a rubber stamp made and stamp in red, "Important; the information you requested". This ensures they will not think it is a mailshot.

This avoids the letter going straight to the bin unread.

If at all possible, avoid address labels as these stink of 'mail shot'. Type the address on the envelope with a printer.

At the end of your letter, guide the reader what to do next, for example:

- you can telephone one of our advisors on 01770654
- email our offices on widgetsrus@net.co
- our fax line is open 24 hours on 01770653
- for more information you may enjoy our local rate 24 hour recorded information line 'widgets in the workplace' on 01770657
- our website is available for your perusal at www.widgetworld.net.co.

See how you *guide* your prospect and not merely dump a load of numbers in a tiny section hidden at the bottom of the page?

Mailshots And Phone Follow-ups

Prospects often need a 'shove' to act on a brochure you have sent, or this may end up in a drawer to be re-visited 'one day'.

A reminder to act is a definition of a mail shot, reminder email, or a phone follow-up. Without these you can possibly halve response in many cases.

Four days after sending a brochure we should make a friendly phone call to ascertain whether it was received. However, we must also ask if there is anything contained in the contents that they would like clarified or whether there was any part of it they would like to discuss.

Gently (and with the emphasis on helping *them* fulfil their needs), initiate conversation about how you can help them.

Phone follow-ups can be very powerful when correctly and thoughtfully done.

Fill the conversation with the benefits of dealing with you and how you would love to be of help to them.

Personalise the call. If it's a prospect that sounds really interested but is teetering a little, perhaps send a complimentary copy of your book? This makes them feel special and gives them the chance to realise you are an author on your subject and to read more information on your company!

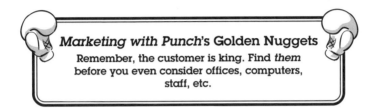

Marketing with Punch's **Golden Nuggets**
Remember, the customer is king. Find *them*
before you even consider offices, computers,
staff, etc.

Try to avoid 'hassling' people on the phone. Make your call very much about *them* and what their *needs* are. I am repeating this throughout the text as it is so bloody important!

Mail shots (or reminder emails), whilst not as powerful as the phone call can be useful, and a good reminder when utilised correctly.

Try to aim your mail shot at the customer's needs and how you can fill this need. Use the mail shot to enquire if there are any questions regarding your brochure or website. It may be prudent to use a postage paid envelope to return this type of questionnaire mail shot.

It may read along the lines of . . .

Dear

We sent you our information pack last week and we would like to know if it met your needs and answered your questions in full.

We have taken the liberty of enclosing a second pack in case the first one got lost in the postal system. [*If the cost of your packs is not too expensive.*]

Your needs regarding the use of our 'super dingly-dangle type II widget' are our prime concern, hence we offer a 100% money back guarantee and free consultation with a widget consultant.

We realise your time is valuable, so may we ask you to let us know if our information is serving you best.

A postage paid envelope is enclosed for your reply.

Name ....

Address ....

....

....

Phone .... Email ....

Fax ....

Questions I would like answered regarding the brochure

....

....

....

(**Alternatively** you may wish to *telephone* an advisor on (01707) 612).

How could ACME Widget Co improve our customer information?

....

....

....

Was any aspect of our information unclear?

....

....

We will endeavour to reply to your questions/comments quickly. Can we reply by phone? Yes/no

Phone no. ....

You may email any queries to us on rogerrammit@widgets.co.net or fax (01703) 4261, Telephone (01707) 612.

Thank you for your time.

Roger Rammit, Senior widget consultant

You have asked an opinion of your customer and automatically they feel 'involved' with your company.

You have also sought to help them even more than just sending a brochure and expecting a response.

This shows a caring company and not only is it more likely to win you custom, but you may learn how to improve the re-run of your brochure or update your website.

Sales calls or mailshots done in this way do not look too 'pushy' or 'salesy', so may benefit when your company has a certain image such as medicine, law, or professions that need a certain 'high-brow' approach.

Alternatively your product may need or warrant a more 'salesy' approach. Ask a question in the headline such as:

- **do you still need a free consultation with our drainage advisor?**
- **is your home still suffering from damp problems? We would love to help you. . . .**
- **did we send you enough information on our language courses?**
- **our trained advisors are waiting to help you with your mobility problems**
- **did you receive your information pack ok? Now we would love to demonstrate a 'missile widget' in the flesh! With no obligation!**

You ask how you can *help* the customer.

Ask them

You may also write and enquire whether they have seen your website or learned anything of use to them from either the site/brochure/information line.

Ask how you can improve on these. People love to give their opinions, and it shows yours as a customer-first company.

Gimmicks

Sometimes a gimmick can work in a mailing. I saw a mail shot sent by HSBC recently, which had a sheet of paper folded into a wallet. When opened it revealed £60 in notes (fake of course!). It went on to ask how would you like this in your wallet instead of paying £60 extra on insurance?

I liked that one! I wonder what response it got?

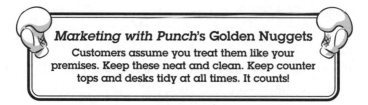

Marketing with Punch's Golden Nuggets

Customers assume you treat them like your premises. Keep these neat and clean. Keep counter tops and desks tidy at all times. It counts!

Back to phone-backs

As we have ascertained the phone-back is king of the **reminders to take action**. There are numerous publications, audios and courses on phone skills, and it is in your interest to suck up as much knowledge on this art as possible.

A major message we try to get across to students of Marketing with Punch during our courses is, we are not the only ones with all the ideas! There are many great writers and marketing teachers out there to learn from. If you can get only one great idea from every book or audio set you listen to, this could be the 'million dollar' clinch!

Email shots

Email shots are used by many businesses where relevant and it's free to use this approach.

When you receive enquires about your company you must remember to obtain all prospects email addresses, to use on your system.

Because of spam filters it may be prudent to make the initial email 'wording only' with a 'link' to a more graphic message, and an instant website link. This way we circumnavigate the filters.

This is one instance where your headline and copy had better be good so the email is not immediately deleted. In other words, use the headline to arouse 'curiosity'.

And . . .

You will have to send email shots more than once! People who get a lot of email almost automatically press 'delete' if a lot of material arrives together. (The same can be said of postal mail shots.)

People receive a lot of spam email nowadays, so again, remember your layout and wording has to be excellent and very relevant in the headline so that it very quickly grabs attention.

Press Releases

It's true to say that our own business launched nationally the day a major newspaper ran a full-page article on us.

Sam had joined in the business as she realised it had a lot of potential, and immediately went about getting a national paper to write an article on our business.

She tirelessly emailed all the national papers and magazines at weekly intervals with a story of our unique position in the market place.

This was not easy as these editors get a lot of stories about companies all vying for space. Using a great headline and her usual brilliant copy writing ours got noticed and used. That was in 2002. This was the true year of achievement!

It is also a good idea when doing press releases to send a copy by 'surface' mail. It's tough to get noticed, but a great *story* will stand far more chance. Like advertising, you must be a sunflower amongst weeds.

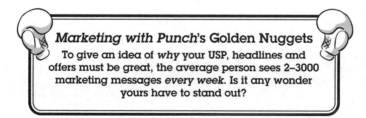

Marketing with Punch's Golden Nuggets
To give an idea of *why* your USP, headlines and offers must be great, the average person sees 2–3000 marketing messages *every week*. Is it any wonder yours have to stand out?

We have deliberately not delved too deeply into PR in this volume, as this subject alone requires its own book.

There are many well-written (and some not so well-written!) books on this subject, but generally this topic requires one piece of advice, which we shall repeat.

No editor will print your press release if there is no story to it.

It is no good sending a story about you having taken on Fred Bloggs (or Joe Schmoe for our American readers), in your accounts department. This is no story for editors and even more non-relevance for readers.

You simply *must* give a reason to run the story.

Editors are constantly looking for good stories as this means they don't have to take up their valuable time writing one!

Do ensure the story goes to the correct department, e.g. a motoring story = motoring editor, a health story = health editor, etc.

Good headlines may be:

- New space age 'toothbrush' makes brushing teeth a thing of the past.
- Local village shop is first to stock 'violent spaceman' computer games (add news of how 20,000 people queued outside all night for a copy!)
- Local author releases charity edition of their book to aid hospice (charity gives you PR leverage every time!)
- Staff at Bryant's builders organise 200 mile hopscotch marathon to help local kids' home.
- 'Man bites dog'. This is an example that has been around since time began, of what editors look for. What it states plainly is that 'dog bites man' is nothing newsworthy, but in reverse, it makes a story. Always think 'man bites dog' when putting out a story.

Many years ago when Les taught sports massage, we organised a massage marathon where people paid £5 for a back massage and all proceeds went to multiple sclerosis.

His qualified former students who got involved handed out their business cards, so they benefited from new clients.

The students got lots of practice, multiple sclerosis received a lot of funding, and the major score for us as a college was . . .

Local papers covered the story before and after, and the local ITV station even turned up on the day to film proceedings for the news.

It was a major success, and Les did not have to advertise the school for a long while!

The manipulation of ideas to promote your company and get press coverage is endless and can be constantly fed by your imagination.

Remember how Richard Branson's round-the-world balloon trips made major headlines in all media for the Virgin empire as a whole? It was unusual, and Branson didn't mind acting the eccentric clown to push the brand awareness of Virgin. He is one clever bastard!!

PR people?

In general we have never found a profession with as many f*****g useless people as PR!

For small businesses these are usually a total waste of money, but . . . there are exceptions. If you can find a PR person to push your company's press releases with genuine passion and gusto. Keep hold of them!*

Obviously you can be your own best PR person, but if you find you do not have the time for this make sure the person is effective. However, the best PR companies tend to have contacts in the press world that you will not have.

Make their results quantifiable and do not settle for endless months of excuses in the "it should appear next week" bracket.

Obviously give them a little time as a good PR person can bring results, but PR is an easy ride-for-money without quantifiable results and you keeping a very close eye on their activities is essential.

---

*See contacts page at the end of this book.

The 'guerrilla' approach

There are some interesting and useful PR concepts under the guerrilla marketing umbrella, and books and audios are available to plough through.

A great example of what we would term a 'guerrilla' exercise was observed by Les at Victoria train station:

It was early January right at the time people book holidays here in the UK.

British Airways holidays sat a lady on a deckchair right in the middle of the station, a cocktail in her hand and holding a large broadsheet newspaper in front of her. The front of the paper, which was in everyone's view, directed people to great holiday offers in the adjacent travel shop.

It was a great juxtaposition on a cold damp day and really got attention. The guerrilla approach probably accounts for more news stories than any other.

Get the story

Do remember at this point to make it easy for editors to carry your story.

They generally need lots of details over and above what you gave in the original story.

You must be contactable, so give your mobile phone number and keep it switched on. If an editor cannot contact the main person, they will simply use a different story where the director was easy to communicate with.

Quite simply, the editor wants to speak to the captain, not the deck hand.

When a story fails and you do not end up in print despite many attempts, try a different approach. Use a new story as the one you chose may not have been as great as you thought.

If Sam had not persisted in our original 'big' story, we may have remained a small local business.

Marketing with Punch's Golden Nuggets
Personal cleanliness and smart clothing are an absolute must in most industries. Would you buy from a person who stank of BO or who dressed like a scarecrow? Nor would we!

Weathering Recessions

During those far off days of running osteopathic clinics, it seemed every clinic we opened was during an economic downturn, and people were not spending.

But, guess what? We out-marketed all the rival clinics in the area every time, and quickly overtook them on client numbers. We were not popular with the other local osteopaths or chiropractors!

During a recession your competition will inevitably cut costs and marketing efforts. They will also cut staff enabling you to poach the best ones.

This is a great time for you as a company to trim your own 'dead wood' from your staff and replace these with more skilled and enthusiastic people.

It is also a great time to pinch market share, as your competition will no doubt trim their advertising efforts. You can literally steal the weaker animals food.

Increase website activity which cuts down press advertising costs.

Use the recession to show people how your company can save them money and time.

Utilise your accounts team and managers by getting them doing phone-backs and general marketing jobs instead of sitting around all day.

Usually you will find that people in the upper brackets will still have money in a recession, but we may need to strategise to attract the lower-class clients to spend on our wares.

Recessions can have their uses, and 'sneaking up' on rival companies is the ideal time for this.

Make It Easy for Your Customer

Doesn't it piss you off when it is difficult to pay for something in a shop, or you are made to jump through hoops to avail yourself of a company's services?

We are the most impatient bastards on God's green earth and we do not wish to use our time being kept waiting, being made to follow company policies (designed to piss us off) or giving money to businesses that do not turn up or are late without a phone call (or don't call us back).

We are not sure whether it's only us, but it seems businesses nowadays like to make things as difficult as possible to trade with them.

Do we resent giving money to these companies? Will we go out of our way to not use them? You bet! One government body that shocked us to the core were the UK passport service. Les lost his passport and urgently needed a new one. He emailed them and within half an hour, had a lovely lady on the phone who got all the documents to him next morning! Brilliant! Now why can't all companies behave like this?

But then two days later a major London department store lost a big sale in an act of sheer stupidity.

Sam filled two baskets with expensive Xmas decorations and queued at the till. Eventually it was her turn. The assistant began to take each and every bauble, star and tinsel piece out and slowly punched the 10 digit code into the till for every individual one. "Its policy" he said. "I'm off" Sam said, and left the whole lot there on the counter top!

Our belief is that if a company makes it difficult for a customer, they need a 'lost revenue' lesson to remind them they have competition.

The easier you make it for your customer, the more money you will make as they will want to use you time and again.

Land Rover

Les is a great traditional Land Rover fan, but realises that in the past Land Rover have struggled on reliability (all this has changed!)

He bought a brand new Defender, and for three years it is covered by a call-out guarantee, much like the RAC, except for Land Rovers only.

He has used it three times, all for very minor things, and the service has been nothing short of spectacular. One call, and within minutes an operator phones back. The call-out guy gets there 'on the dot' of the estimated time and does a brilliant job.

Would he buy another Land Rover? You bet!

Try your hardest to copy this example, it will pay dividends.

The moral is, they make it easy for the customer. Simple!

Top tips on easing your customer's journey (it's worth it)

- Answer phones or return emails quickly. Your competition may be quicker than you and win the sale
- Make it very clear how to contact you in every brochure or web page. Put address, email contact, phone, fax, postal address, out of hours number (if applicable), and of course the recorded information number
- Give a step by step written approach on how to contact you, how to make appointments, where to find you, or seek an estimate, etc, etc.

    The public's general lack of IQ will astound you, and leading them by the hand means even the doziest of people can use you!
- If you have made an appointment at someone's home or place of work, turn up when you say you will or *phone* the prospect.

    If builders and tradespeople knew how much profit they lost by not turning up for job estimates, etc, it would shock them (yes, they are the worst offenders).

    If you are genuinely held up, phone the prospect promptly – you will save around 90% of jobs you may have lost.

- Make it easy to pay. So many shops or companies don't accept debit cards, cheques or cash and just make things hard.

  Here's a warning story for shops who won't take debit cards:

  We were in an Antique shop in Essex where we spotted two pictures at £800. We immediately liked them and went to offer our card.

  "We don't take cards, only cash" the seller said. "There's a cash machine up the road".

  Debit cards have a daily limit on cash withdrawal and we had met ours.

  Next door another antique shop also had a lovely painting in the window, which we immediately liked. They took cards and made a swift sale.

  Two weeks later we drove past the first shop. It had closed down. Be warned!

- If your company employs grey-suited managers who love to make 'company policies' that annoy customers, make sure they run these by *you* first. Entrepreneurs know that making money involves making customers lives *easier*!

35

Understanding The Consumer's Buying Behaviour

Bonus guest chapter by **Paul Williams**

In recent times there have been major changes in the buying public and the way companies respond to this. For example selling has become more worldwide with the advent of easier communication systems – mainly the internet and its derivatives.

Paul Williams on stage

What this has culminated in is simply more customers, higher numbers of sales, lower prices, yet still . . . higher profits!

The consumer has a much greater choice (hence the need to 'niche' market for greater profits), a higher ability to buy, and thus, we have more intense competition.

Many large 'conglomerates' have been replaced by partnerships, alliances and networks, e.g. many banks and building societies have merged in an effort to form one larger bank with more customers. There are many examples of this in other industry types where 'working together' has replaced two hierarchies fighting for custom.

Our traditional marketing culture has always been based around price, promotion and distribution of goods to our *own* culture.

An example of this change in selling products nowadays may be a butcher. He may no longer only sell to traditional English markets, but may have to expand into 90% Halal meats for a growing Muslim community in certain parts of the UK.

Many businesses find they have to appeal to cross cultural diversity in order to satisfy the needs of all customer types. It can be prudent to do your research in this area and the following example is worth heeding.

In an attempt to increase foreign trade, a chosen trade delegation arrived in Taiwan with gifts of green baseball caps.

It transpired that not only was green the colour of the opposition party in their current elections, but, in Taiwanese culture, the wearing of green can denote that the wearer's wife has been unfaithful!

We should also take into account that with the decreasing difficulty in travel, most countries contain a wide range of different ethnic and cultural groups. So it is prudent for the small business to grasp an understanding of these cultural differences as well as the larger more global company.

We can sell more within many companies by understanding the different stimuli that prompt buying in differing culture types.

All behaviour is influenced either by innate influences which may include self-preservation such as eating or nurture which is a direct response to the individual's upbringing and environment. We can safely conclude that we are products of our own past and learnt beliefs. It is in the marketer's interest to understand the development of those beliefs in order to adopt a wise marketing strategy.

Cultural factors

Culture is a major influence in buying behaviour. In a nutshell, culture can be a dominating factor to how your intended customers react to your marketing. After all, culture can be bracketed as the deeply instilled traditions and beliefs that mould us. The basis of most culture is therefore for reasons such as social, hygiene, harmony and the keeping of general codes of behaviour leading to an orderly society.

The reason we need to understand these cultures is that people like and trust people like themselves. This is human nature and we are more likely to buy from people who understand us.

Western culture largely instills beliefs based on values such as achievement and success, material comforts, equality, individuality and health. We pay little attention to these as they are built in to our psyche.

However, in certain cultures the female is suppressed and the male makes all decisions relating to purchases, so this may mean marketing with a 'twist' toward the benefits the male may gain, even from a female product.

Individual cultures may find certain products repellant. Rowntree discovered this with 'After Eight Mints' and the need to persuade the French that a mixture of peppermint and chocolate was not only palatable but enjoyable!

Culture is not static so marketers need to identify cultural shifts in order to create products that meet new waves in thinking and fashion. Western culture has seen a huge shift toward health and fitness, and with this comes a ready market for gyms, healthy foods, low calorie products and illness prevention.

The shift toward informality has opened markets for more casual wear, and the utilization of more leisure time has meant people want convenience products and services such as fast-foods, microwaves, dishwashers etc. It pays to keep a close eye on cultural change patterns by keeping in touch with popular media.

Social class

These days social class divides individuals in society by the sharing of interests, behaviours, living conditions, taste, occupation, income, and their use of money. Class systems differ little in various parts of the world, but differ with the general prosperity of the country.

Developed countries generally have greater numbers of middle class people, whilst undeveloped countries have a working class majority. The attitudes of our class peers can be a major factor in our choice of what and where to buy. This influence can be viewed as somewhat *direct*. For example, a friend of ours with a large majority of working class friends and family became very successful in their business ventures. They keep this hidden from their peers as they feel they will be ostracized for their success.

Class is the reference group that provides people with points of comparison more than any other group. It tends to influence individuals in ways that expose them to new lifestyles, behaviours and experiences. Sharing these behaviour patterns enables the person to 'fit in'. This 'fitting in' creates pressures to conform which will in turn affect their choice of product and brand. For example, this influence is strongest in conspicuous purchases (that which can be seen). This can include clothing labels, certain foods, jewellery, cars and even choices of alcoholic beverages.

People can be influenced by classes they aspire to but do not belong to, and this can be classed as a 'reference group' or 'aspirational group'. A fabulous example of 'aspirational marketing' is Ralph Lauren's 'polo' branding. It exudes polo as a game with its connections to wealth and country lifestyle. People want to buy a 'slice' of this lifestyle, and Ralph Lauren knows this!

Roles in buying products

When buying products, ideas or services the individual will perform that purchase in a differing personal role. Products of personal hygiene will usually be purchased by the individual wishing to use it. Other purchases can be more complicated as they may involve a decision-making process amongst either husband/wife or group members. Generally these purchases are made by:–

1. *An initiator*, who suggests the purchase.
2. *An influencer*, who gives their views and opinions on need or want.
3. *The decider* is the one who makes the final decision after weighing up pros and cons.
4. *The buyer* who buys, but may not have been the decider.

In purchases like these the *user* will be one or all of the group. A domestic appliance, for example, would be used by all of the group.

These roles are dependent on the environment and role the consumer finds themselves in. For example the head of the household such as the dominant parent may make the ultimate buying decision. In the workplace a buyer's role in deciding purchase may be completely reversed.

Other influences

Other influences that influence what and why to buy can include:

1. Age
2. Lifecycle stage
3. Occupation
4. Economic situation
5. Personality
6. Self-concept
7. Domestic outgoings
8. Children or dependants
9. Fixed income e.g. pensioners
10. Lifestyle patterns

Personality types

Personality type throws up an interesting example. Coffee manufacturers discovered that regular drinkers of coffee tend to be more sociable and outgoing personality types. In response to this, the advertising has been devised to show people interacting with one another over a coffee.

Studies generally show that individuals develop their self image based on their role in society and personality traits. Certain possessions reflect people's identities. Those around them view the individual by what they have.

Motivation

Most behaviour is motivated by individual need. Needs occur from both biological and psychological triggers. Biological needs arise from a state of tension such as hunger, thirst and the avoidance of pain.

Psychological needs tend to include the need for recognition, esteem and belonging or acceptance. Once the need reaches a peak it becomes a 'motive'.

According to Freud, the concept of motivation relies on unconscious forces that shape our behaviour. People repress their urges but cannot eliminate them. This can result in dreams, neurotic or obsessive behaviour and at its worst, psychosis. For example a person may buy a guitar and justify this by explaining it as interaction in a hobby. However, Freud's theory would say the unconscious desire behind the purchase was the motivation to demonstrate a creative talent to others. Can you delve deeper and find why *your* customers *really* buy your product?

Maslow's theory offers a hierarchical structure of needs intending to explain why people are motivated by certain needs at certain times. In Maslow's model the first needs to be satisfied are physiological needs such as hunger and thirst. The second are needs for safety that provide the individual with security and protection. Next comes social needs, e.g. the sense of belonging and love. He then explains the next needs are those for esteem such as recognition and status. At the top of Maslow's list are the needs for self-actualisation and realisation; to be all we can be. In this hierarchy of needs each level needs to be reached before the individual could climb to the next. In other words, the need for satisfying hunger and thirst needs to be met before we would be motivated toward satisfying our need for security and protection. Maslow's model is not universal in all cultures.

Perception

A person who has been motivated to act in the satisfaction of their needs is influenced by their own *perception* of the situation. In other words, two people in the same buying situation with the same motivational needs may act differently in their position as potential customers because they perceive the situation their *own* way. For example a television advert may offend some individuals, whereas the perception by a different person may be entirely different and they may find it humorous.

Another example may be that some people could find *Marketing with Punch* offensive with its passionate language and forthrightness. Luckily people who attend our courses love this aspect and find the whole atmosphere and flavour of the courses easy to learn from.

Perception is the result of the individual's reception, organization and interpretation of the stimuli provided from our senses. We must try to cater for these when choosing our type of client base.

Different perceptions of the same stimuli between individuals are created because of three perceptual processes.

1. Selective Attention

This is *very* important to the marketer and goes back to the premise that your marketing must really stand out from the crowd.

With the vast quantities of stimuli that the individual is bombarded with on a daily basis, it is mentally impossible for that individual to pay attention and retain all that has been imposed on them. This means that they will simply discard a very high percentage of what they are subjected to by way of marketing.

Many psychological theories point to a system of filtration used by the brain which 'bottlenecks' messages, allowing some to pass through, and be processed by the brain, and some are filtered out completely.

Give this a lot of thought when deciding headlines in particular. It is so important to stand out!

2. Selective Distortion

People will have generally developed mindsets based on their beliefs, which they will tend to organize incoming information into. Your potential customers will literally adapt your information to their own needs and personal meanings. The information is then interpreted to support what they already believe.

We must think about the mindsets of out potential clients and how they as individuals might interpret our marketing messages.

3. Selective Retention

Much of what we learn is forgotten, and our prospective customers are no exception. We are more likely to retain information that supports our attitudes and beliefs. We also tend to discard bad memories of a product, and retain good ones.

Another example is that we are also likely to remember the good points of a product and forget the good points of a competitor in this field. In other words we like what we know. Because of this the marketer has to work extra hard to get his message across (think USPs[1] and use them!). It is for this reason that repetition plays a big part in advertising, continually reinforcing the message and developing a 'familiarity' that makes potential customers feel safe using our product.

So . . .

a) Use USPs to full advantage.
b) Repeat marketing messages.
c) Use recognizable logos, but realize these are only for recognition building and do not *sell* of themselves.
d) Your product must be brought to the forefront of the consumer's mind by being different and creating mental impact using emotive means.

The decision process

Cultural, social and psychological factors all play an important role in the influence on the consumer's choice of purchase. The marketer will have little influence on many of these factors but provide them with the ability to identify interested buyers and thus the ability to design the company's products to serve their needs.

Now we have established those factors that can be found to affect the buyer's behaviour, an understanding of how the consumer makes their decision to buy must now be considered. This can be viewed in terms of the mental process that the consumer engages in when making a decision to buy a particular product *and* the kind of behaviour engaged in related to the type of purchase to be made.

---

[1]Chapter 3 – (Unique Selling Points) and Niche Markets

A buying decision

It would be easy to simply state the 'whats', 'wheres', 'hows', 'whens' and 'whys' of the consumer decision to buy, and much of this can be gleaned from simple sales figures.

The *actual* reason is in the consumer's thought processes, however. So it is in the marketer's interest to understand, as far as possible, the 'why' of how the consumer came to buy the product. If this can be grasped, we can easier predict the future for our promotions.

It is therefore prudent to understand the five main stages in the decision process.

1. *The recognition of a problem or need to be satisfied*

Firstly the consumer needs to become *aware* they have a problem to be solved. The awareness then needs to become a 'drive' to want the product enough to buy.

2. *The search for information relating to the satisfaction of the need*

Stage two of the decision process is searching for information on the product which satisfies the need or problem of the individual.

If the satisfaction of the need has a significantly high drive then the consumer may purchase what is available immediately to hand for immediate gratification. An example of this may be seen at perhaps the theatre or a concert. The individual is spending time away from their usual environment where there is less choice. Necessarily they will buy whatever is offered at bars or kiosks, not because they have a reasonable choice of price but because of the individual's immediate need to eat or drink. In other words, if the choice is not there, and they have the drive to gratify their desires, they will take what is available. If the drive is not strong enough, they will store the information in their memory to undertake a search in relation to their need.

3. *Sources for the informational search*

When searching for information related to the consumer's interest, the individual will normally relate to a number of sources. These sources vary between the type of product being searched for and the buyer themselves.

Many will initially relate to their personal sources of information which may include family or friends, or those they trust to provide them with fair and relevant opinion. Summing this up, this means they trust those who will construct answers relevant to their lifestyle and enable them to 'weigh up' options.

Other sources of information may be the internet, sales people, advertising copy writing, dealer interaction and image, and brand trustworthiness. The mass media and consumer rating organizations provide the consumer with a public source of information which the consumer can refer to in order to develop their ideas and opinions of the product on offer.

One of the most important sources of information is the experimental source where the consumer gains personal experience of the product, for example a road test on a particular brand of car. A "try before you buy" approach gives consumers confidence in the product. Personal experience is a powerful tool in persuading consumers.

4. Evaluation of alternatives

The next stage in the buying process is evaluating alternative products or services. In this stage the consumer uses the information that they have discovered in the last stage to evaluate the alternative brands in the choice set of the product.

The marketer needs to know how the individual processes the information to arrive at their final brand choice. There is not just one evaluative process consumers go through, but several. By understanding consumer evaluation, our own understanding of certain concepts can be useful.

The first is the assumption that the consumer is attempting to satisfy a need. This would mean that the consumer is in search of particular benefits that acquiring a product would satisfy. The consumer may see several benefits or attributes with varying abilities, allowing the satisfaction of their needs.

The second concept that helps to explain the consumer evaluation process is that the consumer will apply differing degrees of importance to each of the attributes that the product or service may offer. Therefore, different people buy the same item or service in order to satisfy different personal needs.

Salient attributes for the product tend to develop as the consumer thinks about the characteristics of the product. These may not be the most appealing or important attributes to the consumer, but salient because of an advert bringing them to the forefront of a consumer's mind. Further attributes might have been forgotten by the consumer but are actually of importance to them but only recognized when mentioned to them.

As marketers, we must understand the importance of our product's attributes and how these relate to our customer.

Another concept to understand in the evaluation process is the development of brand beliefs. Each attribute of the item is scaled and different beliefs between brands are developed. This is where the importance of brand image comes to the fore. A great example of brand awareness is seen in shops such as Netto or Aldi where some truly great food products are sold very cheaply. The reason for this 'cut-price' approach is that the individual items are generally not marketed as brands and are not recognizable to the public, so the public 'take a chance' on the small unknown brand. In order to sell these, it is done on price alone.

5. There are two factors that stand between the consumer's intention to buy and the actual decision

The first is the attitude of others influencing their choice.

The second factor is situation, such as the price within their income, and of course practicality. For example we may have chosen a two-seater sports car and an unexpected situation arrives such as a pregnancy. The buying decision changes faster than the sports car's top speed, and a seven-seater MPV beckons! Therefore preferences and intentions do not always determine purchase choice.

6. Post-purchase behaviour

Once the consumer has spent their hard earned cash on their product of choice, they will still be evaluating its performance. The consumer will develop satisfaction/dissatisfaction with the product when weighed against their expectations. We obviously want our consumer to be satisfied with their purchase as we wish to encourage repeat buying. We therefore need to pay attention to not raising the customer's expectations beyond the products compatibility.

Buying a new product

When presenting a new product, the marketer needs to understand how the consumer learns about the new product and how they make the decision to adopt the new product.

The adoption process that the consumer goes through involves five mental processes.

1. Awareness – that there is a new product on the market.
2. Interest 'raising' in the product. Increased awareness stimulated by our advertising and marketing.
3. Evaluation – the consumer will carefully evaluate the product and whether it is worth trying.
4. Trial sample – the consumer may purchase the product once or take advantage of a trial.
5. The 'adoption' of the product is the final stage whereby your consumer opts to continue using your product or service.

The job of us as marketers is to help the consumer through the stages of adoption. Using the methods from *Marketing with Punch* this entire process helps you stand out from the myriad of competition out there.

Quite simply, *Marketing with Punch* puts you firmly on the map!

Enjoy your new found success.

The *Marketing with Punch* team

A FINAL WORD

We are confident that you will have found *Marketing with Punch* a great stepping stone to increase your companies profits.

Keep an eye on our website www.marketingwithpunch.com for course details and new ideas.

Alternatively you can phone us on 0208 915 0650 from UK (0044 208 915 0650 USA - overseas).

Marketing with Punch courses run regularly and cover many aspects of boosting your company's profits.

Don't miss out on these brilliant courses . . . your competitors may get there first!

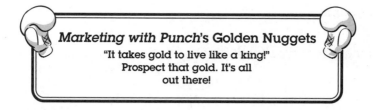

Marketing with Punch's Golden Nuggets
"It takes gold to live like a king!"
Prospect that gold. It's all
out there!

Note – The *Marketing with Punch* team *love* to hear your success stories built from using their techniques. Please email these to us via www.marketingwithpunch.com ("contact" section)

Do you want to learn even <u>more</u> great and powerful strategies?

'Marketing with Punch
.... LIVE!!'

Les Bailey

Sam Williams

Paul Williams

. . . and other brilliant speakers

Courses that boost your business profits into orbit!

Get to one before your competitors do.

For dates go to **www.marketingwithpunch.com**
Int: **0044 208 915 0650**   From UK: **0208 915 0650**

USEFUL CONTACTS

Nightingale Conant

Audio CDs on Sales/Marketing and general self-improvement.

Nightingale Conant
www.nightingale.com

UK customers can request a *full* list of audio programs by phoning 01803 666100.

Highly recommended source for entrepreneurs who wish to make their car or the gym their 'audio university'!

Ted Nicholas books/audios/DVDs

We think Ted is the guru of advertising and direct selling!

Buy all you can of this man's products.
www.tednicholas.com

Printing

Two excellent UK printers we regularly use and enjoy great service from:

Albany Printers
0208 983 8186
www.albanyprinters.co.uk

STR Design and Print
0208 647 9790
www.str.uk.com

UK advertising space

Artavia buy advertising space at preferential rates for companies in all UK newspapers/publications
www.artavia.co.uk
0161 200 8300

DVD productions/TV and general company videos

2020 TV (0208) 662 9999
Contact Rick Barden
www.2020video.tv
www.2020tv.tv

Company law (UK)

Sunil Abeyewickreme
Redwick Legan, Crusader House, 145–157 St John St, London, EWC1V 4PY
(0207) 754 3724

Magazine design and printing

Mandy Lampard at Whoosh design
www.whooshdesign.co.uk

Chartered Accountants

Blythe & Co
www.blytheandco.com
020 8641 6666

Highly recommended!

Photography

Steve Reeve
www.stevereevephotography.co.uk
0785 4651248

Steve undertakes many commercial and product shoots and holds a stock library of 'ready images'. He also teaches at his well-known and respected workshops.

Sound/Audio production (promotional CDs)

Matthew Plumley
www.plumproductions.co.uk.

P.R.

Phil Hall Associates
www.philhallassociates.com
+44(0)207 535 3350

We found this PR company to be very effective: it's obvious they have the press contacts. Recommended!

LOOK OUT FOR OTHER ". . . *WITH PUNCH*" TITLES –

Advertising with Punch
Selling with Punch
PR with Punch

And many others!

CONTACT DETAILS

Marketing With Punch
2nd Floor, 46 Banstead Road
Carshalton
Surrey SM5 3NW

UK: 0208 915 0650
Int: 0044 208 915 0650

www.marketingwithpunch.com